Editor
Lorin Klistoff, M.A.

Managing Editor
Karen Goldfluss, M.S. Ed.

Editor-in-Chief
Sharon Coan, M.S. Ed.

Cover Art
©Susan Winget

Cover Design
Denise Bauer

Interior Art
©Susan Winget

Art Manager
Kevin Barnes

Art Director
CJae Froshay

Imaging
Richard Easley
Craig Gunnell

Product Manager
Phil Garcia

Publisher
Mary D. Smith, M.S. Ed.

Author

Diane M. Hyde

Teacher Created Resources, Inc.
6421 Industry Way
Westminster, CA 92683
www.teachercreated.com

ISBN: 978-0-7439-3075-8

©2004 Teacher Created Resources, Inc.
Reprinted, 2007
Made in U.S.A.

Table of Contents

Introduction 4
Tips for Organization 5
  Introduction 6
  Desk Arrangement 6
  Storage Ideas 7
  Display Space 8
  Hall Passes 8
  Lost and Found Items 9
  Lost Game Pieces 9
  Pencils 9
  Tape 10
  Scissors 10
  Magnetic Strips 10
  Magnetic Business Cards 10
  Dry Erase Boards 10
  Fingernail Brushes and Bottles . . 11
  Markers to Paintbrushes 11
  Student Work Time Music 11
  Calculators 11
  Low or No Cost Items 11
  Filing Cabinet 12
  Envelopes 12
  Contact Paper 12
  Plants on Vacation 12
  Center Organizers 13
  Wallpaper Freebies 13
  Chip Cans 13
  Print Shop Treasures 13
  The Apple Tree 14
  Student Birthdays 14
  Ready for the Rain 15
  Teacher Paperwork 15
  Lesson Plans and Student Work . 16
  Homework Folders 16
  Student Folders 17
  "No Name" Student Paperwork . . 17
  Leftover Worksheets 17
  Recording Student Work 17
  Parent Notes 18
  Chalkboard Lines 18
  Black Line Master Lines 18
  Student Jobs 19
  Student Corrections 19
  The Substitute 20
  Clean Up 21
  Teacher Survival Kit 22
  Teacher "Pick-Er-Upper" 22
  Parent Conferences 22
Tips for Student Behavior 26
  Introduction 27
  Consistency 28
  Documentation 28
  Classroom Rules 28
  Breaking of Rules 28
  General Rules 29

Body Language 29
Learn to Laugh 29
Awards 30
Good Behavior Apples 30
File Folder Rewards 30
Thumbprint Mouse 31
Ticket Rewards 31
Time It 32
Punch-a-Hole Card 33
A Special Meal 33
Red Pen Reversal 34
Tattle-Box 34
Sticker Praise 34
Parent Communication 35
Verbal Praise 36
Special Mailbox 38
It's Awesome! 38
Noise Level Thermometer 39
Classroom Coupons 40
Compliment Box 40
Payday 40
Rewards at No Cost 41
Zip the Lips 41
Fishing on Friday 42
Smile Face Reminder 42
Be Human 42
Silent Signals and Signs 42
Tips for Reading 43
  ABC Order 44
  A-B-C Bags 44
  Match-Up Alphabet 44
  Division of Letters 45
  Sequencing Sentences 45
  Magazine Sequencing 45
  Comic Sequencing 45
  Soup Can Sequencing 45
  Months in Order 46
  Magnetic Cookie Sheets 46
  Fact or Fiction 46
  Braille Alphabet 47
  Classroom Newspaper 47
  Following Directions 47
  "Stump You" Questions 48
  A Special Place 49
  Reading Record Box 49
  "Popcorn" Reading 49
  Cereal Boxes 50
  Stories on Tape 50
  Special Reading Corner 50
  Divide Them Up 50
  Visual Cues 51
  Dictionary Guide Words 51
  Menu Reading 51
  Magazine Subscription Stamps . . 52
  Key Word of the Day 52

Fishing for Sounds 53
Put It Right 53
Catalog Order Form 53
Tips for Language 54
  Window Shades 55
  Vocabulary Illustrations 55
  Mate Search 55
  Puzzle Pieces 56
  Contraction Search 56
  Color Association 56
  Magazine Search 57
  Pantomime Time 57
  Interjections and Exclamation
  Marks 57
  Word Webbing 58
  Word Volleyball 58
  Word Association Game 59
  Oddball Word Association Game 59
  Compound Word Eggs 60
  Plethora of Prepositions 60
  Double or Nothing Compound
  Words 61
  Compound Word Match 61
  Compound Word Art 62
  Compound Go Fishing 62
  Punctuation Action 62
  Dead Words 63
  Observable Opposites 64
  Stirring Up Adjectives 64
Tips for Writing 65
  Which Side of the Paper? 66
  Stringing Cereal 66
  Trace Me 66
  Tile Letters 66
  Brown Bag It 66
  Design a Product 67
  Invent Me 67
  Sentence Expansion 67
  What a Yarn 68
  Fostering Creativity 68
  Class Newspaper 68
  Weekly Writing 69
  Terrible Bs and Ds 69
  Life Timeline 70
  Antonyms 70
  Pretending Time 70
  Invisible Ink 70
  Mail Time! 71
  What Did You Wish? 71
  Alphabetical Order 72
  Writing Time Fillers 72
Tips for Spelling 73
  Star Bulletin Board 74
  A Star-Filled Room 75
  "Sick Words" 75

Table of Contents

Spelling in Braille 76
Spelling with Sign Language. . . . 76
Spelling Demons 76
Add Them Up 76
Stories for Spelling 76
Bong It. 77
Found It! 77
Spell in Clay 77
Glue It 77
Backward Day 77
Spelling Freedom Day 78
Class Response Sticks 78
Type It Out. 79
Write On! 79
Let Me Count the Ways 79
Tips for Math 80
Greater Than/Less Than. 81
Tile Counting 81
Sequencing with Poker Chips . . . 81
Poker Chip Numbers 82
An Addition Bee 82
Subtraction Ruler Tool. 83
Number Flip Chart. 84
Place Value Pockets 85
Place Value Bee 87
Block Dice Place Value 87
Transparency Place Value 88
Door to Rounding Numbers 89
Twos, Fives, and Tens Game 89
Dot-to-Dot 90
Math Baseball 90
Math Magic 90
Roll and Multiply. 91
Multiplication Roll. 91
Multiplication System Idea 92
Hands Multiplication 92
How Much Does It Weigh? 93
Division Chart 93
String Measurement. 93
Teaching Estimation 93
Question/Answer Graphing 94
Weather Graphing 94
Calendar Graphing. 95
Graphing Shapes 95
Play Ball. 95
Odd and Even Days 96
Throw It! 96
Pass It On. 96
Dominoes. 96
Fraction Cue Card 97
Pizza Box Fractions. 97
Plate Fractions. 97
Dig Those Fractions. 98
Restaurant Menus 98
Bargain Advertisements 98

Ad Division 99
Price Power 99
Create Your Own Ad 99
Time Lines. 99
Color-Coded Shapes 100
Oil Cloth Shapes 100
Shape Twister. 101
Shape Bead Necklace. 101
Shape Search 101
Tips for Science. 102
Plants and Growth 103
Spring Egg Planters 105
Terrariums 105
Osmosis in Plants. 106
Weather Vane 106
Teaching Thermometer 107
Tornado in a Bottle 107
Condensation and Evaporation . 108
Volcano Demonstration 108
Snowflake Impression 108
Fossil Creations 109
Rock Hardness. 109
Mineral Content 109
Tips for Social Studies 110
Directions. 111
Atlantic or Pacific? 111
School Map 111
It's That Big? 112
Simon Says 112
Tips for Art 113
Leaf Picture Art 114
Leaf Rubbings 114
Piggy Bank. 115
Tooth Boxes 115
Stained Glass Windows 115
Window Clings. 115
Line Pictures 116
Learning About Color 116
Colors, Colors, Colors 116
Classroom Globe 116
Ice Cream Learning Cones 117
Shape Templates 117
CD Suncatcher. 117
Sewing Cards 117
Bird Feeders 118
Sticker Creations 118
Tips for Centers 119
Introduction 120
Keeping Clean and Neat 121
Storage for Materials 121
Pretend Center: Different Lands 122
Pretend Center: King (or Queen) 122
Pretend Center: Trains and Castles
. . . . 123
Pretend Center: Safari. 123

Pretend Center: Photographer. . 124
Pretend Center: Music Band. . . 124
Pretend Center: Grocery Store . 125
Pretend Center: Playhouse 126
Gardening Center. 126
Poetry Center 126
Reading Center 126
Writing Center 127
Tips for Decorating. 128
Introduction 129
Bulletin Board Backgrounds . . . 129
Bulletin Board Borders 130
Think Color 131
Lettering. 132
Using Hot Glue 132
Hanging from Tiles? 132
Sports Bulletin Board. 132
January: Snowflakes 133
January: Marshmallow Snowmen
. . . . 133
February: Silhouettes 133
February: Valentine's Day. . . . 133
March: Kites 133
April: Spring Flowers 134
April: Butterflies 134
April: Showers 135
April: Sun Catchers. 135
Easter: Hanging Eggs 135
Easter: Coffee Filter Eggs. . . . 135
May: American Flag. 136
September: Ceiling Hangings. . 136
October: Spiders 137
October: Spider Web Board . . . 137
October: Bats in the Belfry. . . . 137
October: Pumpkin Patch 137
November: Classroom Teepee . 138
November: Giving "Thanks" . . 138
Christmas: Suspended Ornaments
. . . . 138
Christmas: Peppermint Special. 139
Christmas: Elves 139
Christmas: Wreaths. 140
Christmas: Student Gifts. 140
Year-Round Seasonal Tree. . . . 141
Colorful Cones. 141
Miscellaneous Tips 142
Symbols in the Directions 143
Which Bus? 143
Which Foot?. 143
Left or Right?. 143
Need a Spinner?. 144
Need More Games? 144

Introduction

All teachers continue to need creative ideas and activities to make learning worthwhile. The purpose of this book is to offer ideas and tips for the classroom and students' learning. These tips and ideas have been selected and designed to arouse students' interest and to create a stimulating learning environment. Many of the ideas and tips come from decades of educational experience.

This book is divided into the following areas:

✓ *Tips for Organization*—In this section, there are many suggestions on how to create a positive and safe environment for your students that will maximize learning. From desk arrangement to cleanup to teacher and student paperwork, the organizational tips will help create a successful environment for you and your students.

✓ *Tips for Student Behavior*—Managing student behavior is a learned skill, but classroom control will begin before the students ever get into the room. This section explains how consistency, documentation, reward systems, and many other ideas can encourage positive student behavior.

✓ *Tips for Reading*—Finding innovative ideas to help students read can be fun. From using cereal boxes to cookie sheets, students will enjoy the process of reading using the ideas in this section.

✓ *Tips for Language*—Want some fresh ideas for teaching words? Here is the section where you will find everything from magazine searches to compound word eggs.

✓ *Tips for Writing*—Getting students to write can be challenging. Tips such as using a mailbox or invisible ink will surely get students motivated to fill their papers!

✓ *Tips for Spelling*—Tired of students' grimaces at the word "spelling"? Well, here are your solutions! Suggestions, such as typing the spelling words to writing them in clay, will diminish the grimaces from your students.

✓ *Tips for Math*—In this section are numerous ideas on how to teach math. For example, place value can be taught with pocket envelopes, dice, or transparency. Read to find out how!

✓ *Tips for Science*—Is teaching science a struggle for you? Read the projects in this section. From a tornado in a bottle to a volcano demonstration, your students will be attentive to your every move.

✓ *Tips for Social Studies*—In this section, there are some helpful hints on how to teach directions and how to learn the location of the Atlantic or Pacific Ocean.

✓ *Tips for Art*—There are some creative art ideas included in this section. From window clings to bird feeders, your students will enjoy their own creations.

✓ *Tips for Centers*—Centers are designed to be teaching areas and are effective, if properly executed. In this section, you will find many ideas for centers and what materials to include in the centers.

✓ *Tips for Decorating*—Tired of the same old things in your classroom? There are many ideas on how to spice up your bulletin boards and create unique and colorful decorations for the seasons.

✓ *Miscellaneous Tips*—Ideas, such as how to teach left and right to students or how to help students catch the correct bus, are included in this section.

Tips
for
Organization

Tips for Organization

Introduction

The way you organize your room is extremely important. Develop your classroom environment to provide quality learning. Here are three important points to remember:

- ✓ Create a positive and safe environment for your students.
- ✓ Create an environment that will maximize learning.
- ✓ Create an environment that will minimize the frequency of behavior problems.

Desk Arrangement

Check these suggestions to include in your decision-making when arranging the desks in your classroom. Remember that the classroom is there for your teaching and the students' learning.

- ✓ Observe how other teachers have arranged their classrooms and choose the arrangement that best suits your needs and goals.
- ✓ Desks or tables might be arranged in one of the following ways: (1) half-circles with a front row and a back row (2) in groups of four or five (3) the traditional way, with chairs lined up, one behind the other.
- ✓ Arrange your room so you can have eye contact with all your students.
- ✓ Arrange your desks so that the students' attention is on the teacher.
- ✓ Make sure that each student is able to see chalkboards and other modes of visuals.
- ✓ Desks should not be placed in front of windows. The glare can be distracting and difficult on the eyes.
- ✓ Note where the "high traffic" areas will be. Try to keep this area free of congestion.
- ✓ Students need to have easy access to those materials that will be used frequently.
- ✓ Students should be able to find their work easily and quickly to promote learning.

Tips for Organization

Storage Ideas

Many things you can find around a home can be turned into school storage. Try using the following items:

- ✓ *coffee cans*—Store small items in these containers.

- ✓ *shoe boxes*—Use these to store science materials for experiments.

- ✓ *skirt hangers*—Use these for holding center materials and posters.

- ✓ *zipper-closed bags*—Use these for games, game pieces, cards, and bulletin board letters.

- ✓ *clear medicine bottles*—Store game pieces in these.

- ✓ *bottle caps and jar lids*—Place small amounts of glue or paste in these for students to use.

- ✓ *cereal boxes*—Cover these boxes and use them as holders for magazines and papers.

- ✓ *clothespins*—Using a hot glue gun, glue clothespins on the inside of your storage closet door. This is perfect for holding all of those bulletin board borders.

- ✓ *plastic butter tubs*—Use these to hold paper clips.

- ✓ *small yogurt containers*—These are good for starting seeds for plants.

- ✓ *detergent boxes*—These can be cut and made into excellent magazine holders for classroom use. Spray paint the box. Then tape the cut rim with plastic tape or electrician's tape.

- ✓ *video cassette holders*—These are great for storage in a student's desk to fend away the clutter.

- ✓ *garbage bags*—If you have trouble with storing large bulletin board materials, try using plastic garbage bags attached to a skirt hanger that holds five to six skirts. You can attach each bulletin board set and store numerous ones on one hanger. Another good idea is to use white garbage bags. You can label each with a permanent black marker for easy identification.

Tips for Organization

Storage Ideas (cont.)

You can also solve some space woes by following this tip. First, get permission from your principal. In many classrooms there is too much dead wall space. Your walls could be filled with plastic rain gutters. Rain gutters can be bought for a small amount of money. They are made of reinforced plastic and can easily be cut into any size piece. You will need plastic brackets to screw them into the wall securely. Here you can display work, put up important rules, or the like.

Display Space

If your display space is limited, try these ideas. Go to your local building supply store. Purchase two lattice panels. Spray paint and join them together with hinges. It can be an attractive addition to your room to display student work, art projects, or posters. It does not cost much to construct and will fold and store easily when not needed.

Another alternative is to purchase a sheet of Styrofoam insulation. This board space will be light to mount on a wall with a hot glue gun.

You can also get a supply of clothespins to use for displaying students' work. You can spray paint them to add color to any display and draw attention to the work.

If you are short on space, here is a way you can hang students' work. Make a hanging board with a piece of cloth and dowel sticks at the top and bottom of the cloth. You might use oilcloth or any other heavier material as these seem to work best. Suspend the cloth board from the ceiling with monofilament line. This board could also work as a divider between center ideas if made wider with double pieces of cloth and longer dowel rods.

Hall Passes

Make hall passes out of poster board (laminated, of course) or have a wood shop teacher make several out of scrap pieces of wood. These passes will be handy—you will not have to stop and write a pass each time. Use cup hangers on your wall to hold all bathroom passes, hall passes, library passes, etc. Place the cup hangers in an area near the teacher work area to make for a secure and out-of-the-way place.

Tips for Organization

Lost and Found Items

Make a lost and found department. Take an old laundry basket and find a place in the room to keep it on hand. Label it "Lost and Found Department." If you find a pencil, lost book, clothing, or any other item that you cannot identify, just put it in the lost and found department. Students will soon learn where to look for things that they cannot find.

Lost Game Pieces

Save plastic milk caps to use for missing game pieces. Decorate them with a permanent marker. Store extras in a covered coffee can (labeled, of course).

Pencils

Do you have students who are constantly losing their pencils? Use a fine point permanent marker to quickly put a student's name on a pencil. Cover the name with clear tape so it will not rub off easily. If a pencil is dropped or misplaced, when found, you quickly know the owner. Placing names on the pencils will save time, especially when pencils suddenly appear on a different desk!

For quick replacement, have a can with extra pencils on the teacher's desk. Label the pencils with your name in permanent marker and cover the writing with clear tape. If, during the middle of the day, a pencil lead breaks, pencils are on-hand at the teacher's desk. If you have pencils that somehow just "disappear" (even with the teacher's name on each), have students sign a checkout card that can be found where the pencil can is located!

As for sharpening pencils, make a class rule that pencils that need to be sharpened should be done either first thing in the morning or before leaving in the afternoon.

Tips for Organization

Tape

The plastic tabs that come on bread and roll bags are handy for tying off the ends of masking tape when you have used it. It is so much easier than having to search for the end!

Scissors

One way to stop losing scissors is to purchase inexpensive cable ties and attach them to scissors. Cable ties can be purchased at any home improvement store. Attach the cable ties tightly and trim the excess cable off. This will help to make the ties permanent. Getting the ties off will be very difficult! You will easily be able to spot which scissors belong to your room. (*Note:* If scissors are dull, keep them sharp by cutting through sandpaper. Works like a charm!)

Magnetic Strips

If you know of anyone who repairs refrigerators or freezers, ask him or her to save all of the magnetic tape that is found around the doors. The cost is nothing, and the rewards for use are great!

Magnetic Business Cards

Many times you will find business cards have a magnetic backing. Do not throw them away. The magnetic strips are perfect for your needs in your classroom. As most classrooms now have white boards that are magnetic, these are perfect for small displays that you wish to put up on your boards during lessons.

Dry Erase Boards

You can easily make a classroom supply of dry erase boards from "shower boards" found at a builder's supply store. You simply cut the board with a jigsaw! These work just like a dry erase board! Another way to make dry erase boards is to use card stock (8 1/2" x 11") and plastic sheet protectors. You can use these as dry erase boards as well.

Tips for Organization

Fingernail Brushes and Bottles

Fingernail polish bottles are good for storing small amounts of glue for project use. The fingernail brushes, themselves, make good paintbrushes for small projects. Just clean them well and they are ready to go.

Markers to Paintbrushes

Most teachers have markers that simply run out of ink and are ready to be thrown away. Do not! Use them for paintbrushes. Works like a charm.

Student Work Time Music

Try playing soft music during a quiet work time. It can work wonders in keeping the classroom quiet and on task.

Calculators

Do you have calculators? In many districts, schools own the calculators. Keep track of the calculators by putting a label on each calculator with a number on it. Stand the calculators in a container so that they stand upright on end. For anyone using a calculator, require all calculators to be checked out on a list and returned to a numerically placed slot.

Low or No Cost Items

You can collect a number of items with minimal or little cost. Many businesses will contribute to students. Many of the large corporations have educational divisions. Write to them asking for a listing of educational materials they will provide for schools. Be sure to use school stationery and the school address. You can get pencils from most banks and armed service recruiting offices.

Libraries can also be of help. Often they have books that give information on free and/or inexpensive materials. One such book is titled *Educator's Guide to Free and Inexpensive Educational Materials.* Your curriculum center will probably have similar books. You can also access information on the Web. There are multitudes of places that offer free materials for the classroom learning experience.

Tips for Organization

Filing Cabinet

A creative teacher will use every bit of space for learning. Attach magnetic tape to the back of lightweight poster board. You can post lists of vocabulary words, words that are often misspelled, instructional signs, or anything that will be of an instructional nature. Attach posters to a filing cabinet. Most file cabinets are metal, so there should not be any problem!

Use the side of the filing cabinet as a drawing or work area. Use blackboard paint on the side of the cabinet. Students can write on it and easily remove any writing.

Envelopes

Did you know that many stores discard extra envelopes from greeting cards that were not sold? Ask if they will save them for you the day that they will be removing and restocking.

Contact Paper

There are so many uses for this product. Yet, sometimes it is difficult to do the job correctly. If you have things in your classroom that you are going to cover with contact paper, it helps to cool the contact paper first. Place the roll of contact paper in the refrigerator for several hours before you use it. This makes it so much easier to use, and it still sticks well.

Plants on Vacation

Do not worry about your plants during school holidays. You can water them and cover with clear plastic bags and make your own miniature greenhouse. If your break is during cold weather, water, and cover the plants, and put them high on a shelf or on the file cabinet. If the heating is turned too low in a building, it could hurt the plant. Just remember that hot air rises and you will probably be safe.

Tips for Organization

Center Organizers

In all centers there must be a supply of materials. One way to organize the materials is to hang a shoe holder on the wall. Label pockets with whatever is needed in a center, such as scissors, stapler, hole punch, markers, and so forth. This way you will not have constant interruption of work.

Think about getting a lazy Susan to go in your art center. Get large-size juice cans, wash them well, and paint them. Spray them with acrylic spray. Glue containers on the lazy Susan and you have holders for just about everything: crayons, rulers, scissors, paint brushes, etc.

Wallpaper Freebies

Never forget that wallpaper stores are a good source of freebies. Ask for out-of-date wallpaper books. These are great for many projects. Use the sheets for picture frames, for bulletin board letters, for art projects, for book covers. It would not be too time-consuming to make journals for students to do their writing activities. Make the covers from wallpaper books and use a sewing machine to sew in the paper. Students could use the "wallpaper" book for a personal journal or to write word lists. If a sewing machine is not available, consider using a hole puncher. Tie the pages with ribbon, yarn, or cording.

Chip Cans

Use those round potato chip cans for activities in the learning center or in direct instruction, either individually or within a group. Cover and label each with the name of the activity. Then, make potato chip shapes to put in the cans. Canned activities could be as follows: number sequencing, alphabet sequencing, alphabetical order, addition and/or subtraction facts, categorization, story or sentence sequencing events. To make these lasting, laminate the shapes.

Print Shop Treasures

Often print shops have leftover paper from some of their projects. Perhaps it is only a small part of the end of the roll, yet, most teachers can find good use for it during craft or art time.

Tips for Organization

The Apple Tree

Consider making an apple tree bulletin board for display during open house. Write items needed for the classroom on paper apple cut-outs. Parents can each pick an apple and this apple will serve as a reminder to parents of how they can help with instruction. Things to consider asking for are as follows:

✓ old video cassette holders for student storage

✓ extra boxes of tissues

✓ paper towels

✓ age-appropriate books for the class library

✓ old magazines for projects

✓ paper plates, utensils, and drinking cups

✓ clothespins for displaying work

✓ a reel of monofilament line

✓ pencils for prizes

✓ Styrofoam peanut packing material

This list is inexhaustible and is only dependent on your instructional needs. Do not get too busy to send thank-you notes to all parents who help. By doing this, you are reinforcing positive working relationships with them.

Student Birthdays

Do you have trouble keeping up with students' birthdays? Use the computer and make a birthday card for each student at the beginning of the school year. This way you can individualize each card. Fold each card and line them up in "birthday order." Store them in a plastic, zipper bag. Make a list of birthdays in order and tape the list to the inside of your lesson plan book. Now you have created a way to keep up and never forget. If you use the computer often, use the free downloads for calendar reminders. A message will be sent to you several days in advance. This will help jog your memory.

Tips for Organization

Ready for the Rain

On days when it rains and students cannot go outdoors, this project can help pass the free time. Purchase oil cloth long enough to make a hop scotch mat. Use permanent markers and the kids are set to go! There is no storage problem as this play mat can easily be rolled up. You can also make oilcloth tic-tac-toe boards using rickrack or other trimming for blocking off spaces. Anything in quantity can be used for markers: bottle caps, milk jug caps, magic marker caps, or pennies. You can paint plastic by mixing a small amount of white glue with the paint and mixing thoroughly. If the paint is too thick, just add water in small increments until you get the consistency you desire.

Teacher Paperwork

With so much to do, it is critical to keep your paperwork organized. How do you keep it all together in one place and know where it is the next time you need it? Use top loading sheet protectors in a notebook. You can load a copy of all worksheets and transparencies and file them away in a specially marked notebook. Classify by units of work. The sheet protectors will not lift the print off your inserts. They also will keep you organized and ready at the snap of a finger!

Another quick way to store work pages or lesson plans so you can readily use them from year-to-year is to use a large magnetic photo album.

New teachers, do everything possible to keep copies of your lesson plans. They will come in handy in the future. Not only can you reuse some of the lessons, but they will also contain tips and teaching techniques that you tried. During any given year, it is wise to jot ideas that you may have heard in the margins. You might want to try some of these ideas for the next year.

Tips for Organization

Lesson Plans and Student Work

Do you have trouble getting it all together and then forgetting where you put it? Try this idea for organizing student work according to your lesson plans. Using file folders, label each folder with the school days of the week. (It is best to make several folders for each day. If you need more, they are already done.) When you need certain worksheets or prompts, file them in the folders that you will keep available on your desk. Be sure that you keep these in the same place at all times. This will also make it easy when a substitute has to come in and take over your class for a day.

If you have the space, use expandable type folders. Make one for each day of the week. The folders can serve the following purposes:

- ✓ hold work missed when absent
- ✓ hold papers needing correction
- ✓ hold special take-home notes and information

Homework Folders

Buy a classroom supply of three-prong/two-pocket folders to be sent home each day. Hold each child responsible for writing down his or her homework assignments each day. (It helps if this is done just before dismissal.) The teacher can go around the room and check to make sure each student has written the date and homework assignment.

Do the following:

- ✓ Write the student's name on the folder.
- ✓ Write "Return" on the left pocket of the folder.
- ✓ Write "Keep" on the right pocket of the folder.
- ✓ Secure notebook paper under the prongs.

On the "Return" side, you will put all papers that need to be sent home for parent signatures and homework. The "Keep" side is to remain at home.

 # Tips for Organization

Student Folders

Have trouble keeping up with makeup work for absent students? Have trouble keeping up with the individualized work? Try this idea. At the beginning of the year, make each student a pocket folder with his or her name written on the front. Place a file box in a place accessible to all. Teach your students to get their folders when they first arrive in the morning.

"No Name" Student Paperwork

Hang a lightweight cord across one of the walls of your room. Obtain brightly colored clothespins. Then, when you receive a paper without a name, hang the paper on the line. Even if you know to whom the paper belongs, hang the paper anyway. It makes for a good, unspoken reminder to always put your name on the paper!

Another idea is to have a box where students will put all work that is to be turned in to the teacher. Using string, tie a highlighter to the box. Students are told that they must highlight their names before turning in their papers. Students will love this idea!

Here is another suggestion. Wherever you have the "no name" work, why not have a "Mr. No Name" paper character. Put all work without names in a box under Mr. No Name.

Leftover Worksheets

What can you do with all those extra worksheets? Make a free-bee can by taking an empty coffee can and covering it. Decorate the can and add in bold letters: FREE—JUST FOR YOU. Let students take the extra worksheets to do the work or just to draw on the backs when they have completed their work.

Recording Student Work

An easy way to know that you have recorded student's work is to clip the corners of the pages. It also informs the parent that this recorded work is part of his or her child's grades for the grading period. Some teachers prefer to simply make a mark in the corner. Others like to draw a smiley face in the upper right-hand corner!

Tips for Organization

Parent Notes

With primary students, you often question whether the notes ever get home to the parent. Here is an idea to foster their return. Order address labels, but instead of putting your own name and address on these, follow this suggestion:

First line: Attention
Second line: Please sign
Third line: Return to teacher

Be sure to inform your parents at open house that this is what you plan to do. You will gain parental support.

Another idea to encourage the return of papers is to have a special folder in which to keep work for signatures. Have the folders all be the same color and put one of the "address" labels on front of each.

Here is another idea that is worth the try! When you have a note to send home to parents, fold the note into a wristband to put on the student. Seal it with a sticker.

Another idea is to cover and decorate potato chip cans to carry notes. Label the can with the child's name and attach a cord so it can be hung around the neck. Be sure to remind parents to return your "note box"!

Chalkboard Lines

On the chalkboard, try making your lines with poster paint. You can write with chalk over the poster paint line without it coming off. Then, whenever you need the lines taken off, just wash with warm water.

Black Line Master Lines

Do you need to make work sheets that require straight lines? Get a tracing wheel that is used in sewing. You can make straight lines by applying lightly, using a piece of notebook paper for a guide.

Tips for Organization

Student Jobs

Have students apply for jobs around the classroom. Develop student jobs such as the following:

✓ office messenger   ✓ room detail agent

✓ morning teacher helper   ✓ teacher messenger

✓ board keeper   ✓ work collector

✓ afternoon helper   ✓ board erasing maintenance

✓ line leader

Have students apply for bi-weekly jobs. Have the students fill out applications for the jobs. Have an interview with each applicant, and ask the student to tell why he or she is suited for the job. Emphasize the need for correct behavior in qualifications for the job. Talk about how important the job is and how the person who has the job is being counted on to do his or her very best. Post the names of students who have "won" the particular jobs. Expect all students to participate. Students will learn to complete forms, how to sign their names, etc.

Student Corrections

All students miss things or make mistakes on their work. Do they seem embarrassed when you return papers for correction? Do they rebel against the idea of correcting the errors? Try making a "mistake magnifier." This idea promises to be an unobtrusive way of letting a student know to recheck a paper. Follow the directions below to make your "mistake magnifier."

1. Out of card stock, cut out two "magnifiers" which are the same size.

2. Draw two large, same-sized inner circles on the "magnifiers."

3. Cut out the inner circles.

4. Glue cellophane between the two circles.

5. Glue all parts together to make your "mistake magnifier."

Use the "mistake magnifier" to clip to papers needing correction. Be sure to place a box in an area where students can return the "mistake magnifiers."

Tips for Organization

The Substitute

There are times when you will not know, in advance, that you will be absent from your job. There may not be enough planned for a substitute. Having a substitute folder is definitely a plus. Make one that you can keep in your desk drawer or in a special spot with your lesson plan book. Inside the folder you should include the following items:

- ✓ class list and seating chart

- ✓ class schedule

- ✓ brief description of your duties and the days you have duty—i.e. lunch, dismissal, before school

- ✓ list of dependable students to carry a message to the office or another teacher

- ✓ description of your daily routine, such as how you take up lunch monies, how students should be dismissed, manner in which the office can be reached in case of emergency

- ✓ notes about the discipline/management system

- ✓ special notes on any student behavior

- ✓ special information on students—such as frequent need for bathroom or medication given at office

- ✓ names of all the staff or names of teachers in the area

- ✓ substitute time fillers and special work

- ✓ stickers or special treats for good behavior

- ✓ an evaluation form for the teacher to fill out

The substitute will appreciate all the information and you will not have to worry about your lesson plans and how the day is going. Your lesson plans should be as complete and clear as possible. Note where books can be found and on what pages the lessons are found. Also, make a note as to whether or not you want your substitute to grade papers and designate a spot for them to be placed once they are finished.

Tips for Organization

Clean Up

It is always time-consuming to have to clean up, but it must be done. Here are some tips on cleaning.

✓ Silver polish will take off grease pencil marks.

✓ Toothpaste is great for cleaning wooden desks, especially those water spots.

✓ Shaving cream also cleans wooden desks. Not only will the students have a blast using it, but they can finger-paint and make designs as they clean. (*Note:* With small children, be sure to put newspaper on the floor under the desks.)

✓ For reviving old blackboards or chalkboards, just put a little Murphy's Oil Soap® in a spray bottle, spray on boards, and rub in.

✓ When you are doing class artwork and dread the mess, cover the worktables with old newspapers.

✓ When using tempera paint, try filling empty roll-on deodorant bottles with the paint for easy painting.

✓ Baby wipes are wonderful for wiping hands when needed, cleaning up the room, cleaning dry erase boards, cleaning spills in the room, getting off pencil marks on desks, and erasing transparencies. Not only do they smell good, they are non-toxic.

✓ Tissues with lanolin make good wipes for all chalkboards.

✓ Hair spray cleans dry erase boards and will get ink out of clothing. It also removes permanent marks from furniture. If the hair spray seems a bit sticky, spray with rubbing alcohol and wipe.

✓ For removing crayon marks, just use baking soda and water and rub away.

✓ Some teachers keep a spray bottle of water and a roll of paper towels by the overhead projector for cleaning the transparencies. Other teachers have suggested covering the original transparency with plastic wrap and writing on it, rather than on the original transparency. Then, just throw the plastic wrap away.

✓ W-D 40 is excellent for getting tape off walls or boards or project work.

Tips for Organization

Teacher Survival Kit

Considering that teaching is often a very taxing job, all teachers need to have a survival kit. A survival kit will remind us why we chose to be teachers. Include in your kit the following items (*Note:* Phrases taken from a poem by an unknown author):

- ✓ A pencil so you can write down your blessings

- ✓ A piece of chewing gum to help you remember to "stick with it"

- ✓ An eraser to help you remember, everyone makes mistakes, even teachers

- ✓ A candy kiss to help you remember that we all need hugs now and then

- ✓ A toothpick to remind you that you can pick out the good things in anyone

- ✓ A smiley face to help you remember a smile takes less muscles than a frown

- ✓ A seed to remind us that things grow and mature and things can change

Teacher "Pick-Er-Upper"

Sometimes teachers need a bit of pepping up. Try this idea for a teacher friend. Obtain several medium-size empty pill bottles from the local pharmacy. On a large adhesive label, write the "prescription" below for a teacher friend or other co-worker. Paste it to the pill bottle. Fill the bottle with some type of small candies. Place it on a friend's desk or in his or her mailbox. Just the idea will help brighten the day!

RX# 12345	100 mg
Dr. (your name)	For: (Whomever)

Directions: Whenever you are feeling down in the dumps, take one or two of these for an energy boost. Refill as necessary.

Parent Conferences

The time has come for parent conferences. How can you make any conference successful? Parent conferences can be a pleasurable experience where teacher and parents can interact. To ensure a positive outcome to the conference, follow these tips.

Parent Conferences *(cont.)*

Prior Communication—Some teachers find it effective to make a brochure to give parents at the beginning of the school year. What should you include in a brochure? Here are several suggestions:

- ✓ a list of class rules
- ✓ homework requirements
- ✓ a time schedule of daily activities
- ✓ expectations of times you will be free for telephone calls or conferences
- ✓ principal's name, assistant principal's name, school telephone number
- ✓ Never put your home telephone number in a brochure. You may not want parents (or students) to call at home. Use discretion and only give out the number when you know it will be kept in confidence by the parent.

At the first of the year, before the formal conference time, call the parents. Get off to a good start with your parents. Call and introduce yourself as their child's teacher. Tell about things that are happening and will be happening in the classroom. Find something good to say about their child. You will not only aid in fostering a positive relationship with the parents, but it will make it easier to work with them during conference time. Too often, teachers do not make an initial contact prior to meeting them for the first time at parent conference time. Prior contact pays off dividends in the long run.

Inviting Parents—When the time comes for setting up the formal conference period, ask both parents of each child to come. This affords you the opportunity to meet both parents and helps to clarify questions they might have. Remember, your school year will be more successful if you have the parents backing you and believing in you. Most of the time, you will find parents cooperative and willing to help in any way. However, be prepared. You will have some parents who are hostile. Do your best to make them feel comfortable by listening to whatever they want to say. If you get defensive, you will only complicate the issue. Try to offer ways to correct any problem that may be brought into the conference.

Tips for Organization

Parent Conferences (cont.)

Prior to the Conference—Be organized and do the following:

✓ Have ready a folder with samples of the student's work.

✓ Have your grade book and grading scale readily available if needed. (*Caution:* Be sure to be cautious enough not to show any other student's grades. When parents are able to see other students' grades, you will be breaking any rule of confidentiality.)

✓ Know the questions you want to ask that will help you to work with their child. Think carefully over any questions you have that might be personal. You do not want to probe into personal affairs. Also, be sure to ask and listen to the parents' opinions. And, by all means, never be judgmental, for your goal is to form a positive and productive working relationship.

✓ Arrange your conference area where there are no physical barriers that would come between you and the parent. It makes for a more comfortable discussion environment. For example, do not sit behind your desk. You want to meet the parents on an equal basis. It is necessary to make them feel comfortable and at ease.

During the Conference—Be organized and do the following:

✓ Greet the parents at the door, welcoming them into "your turf." Remember that it is very important to make them feel welcome and comfortable.

✓ Watch your body language. Research has shown that body language sometimes speaks louder than words. The non-verbal cues that you emit will often set the mood of the conference. You want the parent to realize that you are interested in their child and what they have to say about their child.

✓ Be specific in what you want to say to the parent. Do not flounder.

✓ Do not use educational jargon that the parent may not understand. Talk in layman's terms. You want to ensure that they completely understand all that you say.

Tips for Organization

Parent Conferences *(cont.)*

✓ Focus on the strengths of the student first. Parents want to hear good things about their child. Later, you may feel more comfortable addressing any areas where the student is having difficulty or creating problems. Remember that it is always wise to focus on a solution to any problem rather than focusing on the problem itself. Discuss the problem. Ask the parents to give suggestions as to how the problem would be best served. You want to work together with the parents in the remediation of any problem.

✓ Help parents feel free to ask questions. Be prepared for possible questions the parents might ask such as "How is my child doing in school?", "What are his or her grades?", "How can I help him or her do better?" "Have you had any problems with his or her behavior? If so, what will you do to solve the problem and how can I help support you in this?", or "What are your discipline procedures?"

Ending the Conference—Whatever you do in your conferencing with the parents, you want to end the conference on a positive note. You need to have secured their cooperation and their support.

Record the Conference—Always make a record of the parental conference. You will need to allow time, after the conference, to immediately make notes of what transpired. Be sure to schedule plenty of time for the conference. File all notes individually in each student's personal folder. The importance of documenting everything in your work cannot be emphasized too much. You never know when such documentation may be needed to back up your position. Do not take lightly the documentation of conversations, notes, conferences, and student behavior.

Other Tips—Be sure that whenever you are sending information or notes home to the parents, you have used correct grammar and spelling. You need to write any message clearly and concisely. Be neat in your work as it is a reflection of you as a teacher and the educational system. Always keep a copy of any communication you have with any parent, such as notes that were sent home or telephone calls.

Tips
for
Student
Behavior

Tips for Student Behavior

Introduction

Good discipline does not just happen all at once. Managing student behavior is a learned skill, but classroom control will begin before the students ever get into the room. It is no easy task. Each teacher will develop his or her own form of discipline. Remember that students need to feel valued and welcomed. They need to know that you have an honest interest in each one of them, not only as a class, but also as individuals. For good discipline, certain behaviors are necessary on the part of the teacher:

✓ Be consistent; establish the rules and stick to them.

✓ Consequences should be fair and consistently applied.

✓ Be prepared for the students who will test the rules.

✓ Do not threaten students with a consequence unless you are ready to carry it out. Students will view you as inconsistent if you fail to do what you say.

✓ Do not be judgmental; look at each situation from all angles before you designate a consequence.

✓ Never put off discipline. Handle any behavioral problem when it occurs.

✓ Make sure students understand the rules and the consequences. Students need to know how to behave in any given situation. With some students, you may want to do role-playing at the beginning of the school year. In this way, students will see what is expected of them and see the consequences being applied.

✓ Show a true interest in all of the students. Each one needs to be treated as an individual and with respect, not just another student. When giving praise to any student, use his or her name with the praise. Nothing pleases students more than to hear their names used in a good light.

✓ Implement well-planned lessons. Know what you are going to teach and be well prepared.

✓ Allow for flexibility. There will be many interruptions in a school year; you will not accomplish everything that is planned on a particular day.

Tips for Student Behavior

Consistency

This is extremely important in controlling your classroom. Enforce all rules fairly and consistently. To become consistent, you need to remember to be objective in any situation. It is easy to be judgmental, but this is only a detriment to consistency. You need to look at all issues and evaluate each issue individually. You need to be fair, positive, and most of all, consistent.

Documentation

Keeping documentation when negative behavior occurs is not only smart, but useful for evaluation. You should keep the date, time, and incident on record. Additionally, you need to include how you handled the situation and what occurred. Be brief, but be complete. One way to record is to maintain a recipe box where you have filed cards labeled with student names. When a disruptive behavior occurs, jot it down to be recorded later.

Classroom Rules

Post classroom rules and make sure that your rules are consistent with both the school building and school district policies. Discuss the rules and their consequences with the students. It is your responsibility to make sure that the students understand each rule. Students need to know the rules for classroom behavior and the consequences of breaking the rules. In good teaching, the teacher does not make idle threats. Remember that there will always be some students who will try the teacher and the rules. A teacher must be prepared for these students. It will happen.

Breaking of Rules

What should you do when a student breaks a rule? First, do not put off the consequences. You need to address the infraction immediately and directly. If not, the problem that occurred may expand into a larger problem. Secondly, if you were to put off addressing the problem, the behavior and its consequences are minimized.

# Tips for Student Behavior

General Rules

Be sure that your students understand the following:

- ✓ what to do when someone knocks at the door
- ✓ how and when to throw away trash
- ✓ how to exit the classroom in an orderly fashion
- ✓ what to do if pencil lead breaks
- ✓ what to do in a fire, earthquake, tornado, or hurricane drill
- ✓ how you want papers turned in
- ✓ what to do when late for school
- ✓ what to do when work is finished

Body Language

Think of using body language to control students. Rather than orally disciplining, body language can be utilized. There are times when a mere signal will be effective. For example, if the room is too noisy, raise your hand. Wait until the class notices and everyone follows you, raising their hand.

Other body language signals include the following:

- ✓ a tap on desk = "check this"
- ✓ thumbs up = "very good"
- ✓ touching chin with fingertips and moving downward = "good for you"

You can use your body to define use of space. Students feel more accountable the nearer you are to their space. Many times, your physical presence and proximity will stop a behavioral problem from occurring.

Learn to Laugh

Laughter is a good antidote to any situation when applied appropriately. All teachers need to learn to use appropriately-applied laughter as a resource.

Tips for Student Behavior

Awards

At the beginning of the year, talk to the students about what happens when they get report cards. Set up a system by which you can present award certificates at the end of each reporting period. For example, you can give certificates for the following:

✓ kindness certificate	✓ neatest desk
✓ improved behavior	✓ turning in all homework
✓ good behavior	

Students love to receive awards. Awards help parents to know what is happening in school. Also, students like the positive attention. Be sure to make awards that are attainable by all of the students. You need to keep a record of the awards given so that you do not give some students awards too freely. All students need a goal to work toward.

Good Behavior Apples

Reward good behavior. Make a list of things you wish to reward such as completing work, neatness, bringing back homework, showing a special kindness, etc. Then, cut an apple pattern for each child. Label each apple with the student's name. Post all apples in a special place in the room. When things are rewarded, take a "bite" out of the student's apple by hole-punching the apple. When the apple is "eaten," have some type of a special reward.

File Folder Rewards

Develop a file folder for each student. Block off sections on the inside of the file folder in 1/2-inch squares using a marker. If the student has done very well on an assignment, shows kindness to another, follows instructions well, or other such actions, draw a smiley face in one of the blocks. When the student has filled his or her file folder, allow the student to have a special treat. Let the student choose among such activities as free time, working with a partner, being the teacher helper, etc. Treats should be decided according to age-level appropriateness.

 # Tips for Student Behavior

Thumbprint Mouse

Parents want to know how well their children are doing. One cute way for the teacher to put a special touch to papers is to make a thumbprint mouse on a well done paper. Use an ink pad and make your thumbprint. Then use a fine tip marker to make the eyes, ears, tail, and a great bit smile!

Ticket Rewards

An excellent way of encouraging good learning behavior is a reward system. This one has proven to be of top-notch value. Go to a party store (or to a school catalog) and purchase tickets similar to the ones used in carnivals and at the movies. Give a ticket for the behaviors you wish to reward. Have the student sign the back of the ticket and drop it in a "prize jar." At the end of each week, have a drawing for a special prize. At the end of a grading period, throw out all tickets and begin again. This gives all students a chance for improving behavior and learning.

Set the limits for all students. Explain that some things one student needs to learn or do may be different from a goal that you want another student to learn or do. Remind them that there are differences in all people. In this way, if you have explained well enough, you can give rewards for small steps in one student and not to another.

Students love to catch the teacher making a mistake. Challenge students to find a mistake you make. The first one to find the mistake gets a ticket to put in the ticket drawing jar (for surprises at drawing time). Deliberately make at least one mistake a day to keep students on their toes.

(*Note:* It is best to be conservative at first. Students need to learn that anything worth having is worth working for. Too many tickets will dilute any learning experience that you may want to have. The rewards you give each week do not have to be grand—it is just the fact of winning. It may be pencils, rulers, or yo-yos. Just winning puts that extra smile on a student. The drawing of tickets also gives the student who has not earned many tickets a good chance to win. You may find that this idea is better than having the student purchase a prize at the end of some given period.)

Tips for Student Behavior

Ticket Rewards *(cont.)*

Some ways to earn tickets are as follows:

- ✓ any paper with a 95% or above
- ✓ a perfect spelling paper on the trial test
- ✓ a specific helpful kindness someone does for another
- ✓ bringing in homework all week
- ✓ bringing in signed papers
- ✓ turning in all library books on time

Ways to lose tickets are as follows:

- ✓ being disruptive in any part of the school
- ✓ loud fussing or any fighting
- ✓ running in the hallways
- ✓ playing in the bathroom
- ✓ arguing with others or not sharing

When grading a paper and the student has a 95% or above, go ahead and staple the ticket to the top of the paper. This will save you time and effort. It should be the responsibility of the student to write his or her name and to deposit the ticket in the jar. This is merely teaching responsibility.

This ticket idea, with the earning and losing of tickets, also works well with older students using play money. It is a bit harder, though, for some students to keep up with their money, but using money can be expanded to enrich the math curriculum. Each month, supply each student with a paycheck in the form of paper money in different denominations. Set up ways to increase earnings and to decrease, or lose, monies they have.

Time It

Here is an idea that works for some teachers. Obtain a silent kitchen timer that has a buzzer. Set the buzzer to go off. When the buzzer goes off, catch a student being good!

 # Tips for Student Behavior

Punch-a-Hole Card

Need a way to reward good behavior? Make a card for each student and divide the card into small squares, large enough to place a hole punch. Randomly give punches to student's card, ensuring that the student realizes that he or she has earned the reward. Keep the punch card in a visible place on the student's desk. In this way, you can check to make sure that you are not missing a student or unfairly giving one student too many punches on his or her card. Randomly reward behaviors such as the following:

- ✓ completing work assignments
- ✓ following instructions well
- ✓ studying with another student
- ✓ attention to task
- ✓ helping another student
- ✓ showing kindness to another

Consider using one of the newer specialty design punches, such as shapes like stars or hearts, rather than using the ordinary hole punch. Additionally, set a time limit on the card's use, such as a card for every two weeks, or so. You will find that students will count the number of holes they have earned. This makes the card a constant reinforcer of good behavior.

(*Caution:* The good student will typically earn hole punches too quickly. Therefore, make sure that these types of students do things over and above the behaviors they normally exhibit. Therefore, you are setting a goal for the good student to achieve.)

Have a special reward or treat when each student has earned a set number of hole punches. Students must know they are working to attain a goal. The goal should be within reason.

A Special Meal

One treat you can use is to allow a student to choose to eat with you alone. This can make for a very special lunch. You might eat in the classroom without other students or in a special area in the lunchroom. Remember, it is a special occasion.

Tips for Student Behavior

Red Pen Reversal

Teachers often use a red pen to mark answers that are incorrect. Instead of using a red pen to check all wrong answers, use a red pen to check all right answers! Write "okay" on all correct answers. Leave answers that are wrong untouched. This is another silent message to students to go back and correct the wrong answers. They know, without you saying, that the problems are wrong, and they know which problems to correct. Be sure to use a red pen or pencil. Students have learned to associate red marks with the word, "wrong." Using a red mark for the right answers is a way of using reverse psychology on them.

Tattle-Box

Tattling can be a big problem in a classroom. This type of behavior usually occurs when a student is trying to gain teacher attention. Students can tattle for the following reasons:

✓ to get others in trouble

✓ to hopefully get an award

✓ to gain attention

✓ to feel superior over others

Try using a tattle box. Cover a shoebox with paper. Label it, "The Tattle Box." When a student tries to tattle, have the students write the problem down on paper and drop it in the box. Be sure to keep paper and pencil handy beside the box and be sure to read the papers!

Another tactic to curb tattling is when a student comes to tattle, ask a question: "Is it in or out?" In other words, you are asking the student "Are you tattling to get someone in trouble or out of trouble?" Only listen to those who say "out of trouble." Students catch on quickly that you are not going to listen to their negative tattling. (*Note:* Remind yourself not to get irate when something happens. Announce, "Okay, who did this?" Try to set a good example.)

Sticker Praise

Mark extra good work with a smiley sticker and watch the smiles on students' faces. It is simple, but it works.

Parent Communication

If you want to establish good communication with the parents of your students, call each one at the beginning of the year. Talk about his or her child and say some positive things. Having good communication with the parents is extremely important. When you have to call to report some type of negative behavior, it is much easier and acceptable. You surely do not want to start off the year with a negatively charged classroom!

You need to be positive in your reports to parents. As stated, you not only want, but need, good parent rapport. In writing notes to parents, try to use positive comments. Turn your statements around to your benefit. Use statements such as the following:

- ✓ cooperative
- ✓ willing
- ✓ is strong in
- ✓ has a good grasp of
- ✓ is attempting
- ✓ is striving
- ✓ does a find job with
- ✓ excels in
- ✓ is making good progress

Avoid negative words and statements such as the following:

- ✓ is not able
- ✓ will never
- ✓ won't
- ✓ can't
- ✓ doesn't
- ✓ will seldom

Tips for Student Behavior

Parent Communication *(cont.)*

With students who have behavioral or academic problems on which you need to comment, use statements such as the following:

- ✓ needs help with
- ✓ will need your help to
- ✓ strives hard to
- ✓ needs reinforcement
- ✓ could profit from
- ✓ sometimes finds it difficult

Do not just put down anything. Think before you write. Parents need to be kept informed of any problems. Be sure, however, that you have contacted the parent prior to progress report time. Do not surprise the parent. Parents have a right to know how their child is doing and where help is needed. As time consuming as it is, asking parents to come in to visit before or after school will pay off dividends in the end.

Verbal Praise

You do not always need to give away a treat. Learning verbal praise is not as easy as it sounds. Yet, the more you praise, the easier it gets to put this tactic into your teaching. A healthy dose of praise works wonders.

Disruptive classroom behaviors do not go away like magic. It takes both time and practice on the part of the teacher. Praise is very effective if it is used appropriately. Students will know if the praise is not sincere. The following are some examples of verbal praise:

- ✓ Way to go!
- ✓ Keep it up!
- ✓ What good work!
- ✓ Top-notch!

Tips for Student Behavior

Verbal Praise *(cont.)*

- ✓ That's great!
- ✓ Right on!
- ✓ Great work!
- ✓ I am so proud of you.
- ✓ Wonderful!
- ✓ Fantastic!
- ✓ Super-Duper!
- ✓ You make me proud!
- ✓ How about that!
- ✓ Far out!
- ✓ Super work!
- ✓ Wow!

Read the following list to get an idea of things for which you can praise a student:

- ✓ taking turns
- ✓ listening well
- ✓ having all materials
- ✓ helping a friend
- ✓ using good manners
- ✓ keeping busy when work is finished
- ✓ asking questions when things are not understood

- ✓ participating in a lesson
- ✓ learning a new skill
- ✓ being on time for class
- ✓ staying on task
- ✓ entering room quietly
- ✓ returning materials

(*Caution:* You can cause more problems if you praise and it is not deserved. Be honest and forthright. Give praise to all students, not just the ones who make the best grades. You have students who may be working up to their abilities, but not to the grade level of other students. These students should get an A for effort and praise for trying.)

Tips for Student Behavior

Special Mailbox

A cute idea for the classroom is to mount a real mailbox on a support stand. Use this to send special notes to students, praising their efforts and progress.

Some examples of reasons to send notes are as follows:

- ✓ being kind to another
- ✓ making learning progress
- ✓ being polite and courteous
- ✓ birthdays or other special times
- ✓ putting away something left out
- ✓ cleaning up unprompted
- ✓ saying something kind
- ✓ helping another student
- ✓ straightening the desk
- ✓ remembering what the teacher said

The teacher can write a special note to the student who is caught being good and put it in the mailbox for delivery. Have a mailman deliver the notes at the end of the day. Students love getting their mail and showing it off to others.

You can also have note cards ready for others to write notes. The principal, another teacher, the lunchroom people, or the custodian might want to offer praise. You can attach a small piece of magnetic tape to the back of the note before you send it home. Parents love knowing the good things their child does and posting the evidence on the refrigerator.

It's Awesome!

After students know and understand rules and consequences, this idea will work with success. Cut out the letters for the word, *awesome*. Attach each letter to a visible board at the beginning of the week. Tell students that if they can keep up the word all week without losing all the letters, there will be a special surprise on Friday. When disruptive behavior occurs, remove one letter. Continue to remove letters whenever necessary. You will be surprised how much peer pressure works.

Tips for Student Behavior

Noise Level Thermometer

Make a large thermometer to control the noise level in your room. Mark it with the same temperature marks as those on a real thermometer. Use a red ribbon for the mercury. Begin each day with the room thermometer set on zero. When the noise rises, raise the temperature. The consequence of having to raise the temperature needs to be established and agreed upon by the class. Make it a cooperative learning experience.

Follow the directions below to make the noise level thermometer.

1. Using poster board, cut to rectangular size desired. Size should be large enough to be seen by all students.

2. Make slits approximately one inch from the top and one inch from the bottom of the poster board.

3. Cut a strip of ribbed ribbon long enough to go from the top slit to the bottom slit.

4. Insert the ribbon into one slit area.

5. Attach elastic to the ends of the ribbon so that the ribbon and elastic are sewn together for movement of the mercury.

6. Mark the temperature degrees as on a regular thermometer.

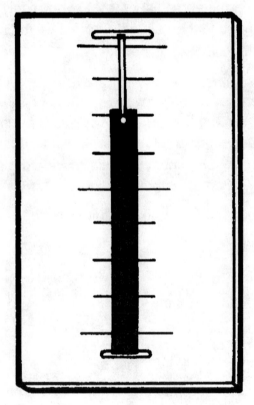

Tips for Student Behavior

Classroom Coupons

Why not create coupons to give as rewards for good behavior, special efforts, good work? Coupons could be for eating with the teacher, a night off from homework, having lunch with another class, moving one's desk to a preferred spot, etc. Coupons are a fun way to reward.

Compliment Box

Have a special box for just compliments. Encourage students to write a compliment when they catch a classmate doing something nice. At the end of each day, read each note aloud and then, give the notes to each student who was complimented. This tactic can build up students' self-esteem. You might want to keep a list of those who receive notes in order to make sure that each student gets a note from time to time.

Payday

To make this technique work, you must have a pocket folder for each student. On the first day of a two-week period, students are given a set of homemade money, cut and stapled in a durable envelope with their names on the front. Students will, initially, write their names on the back of the money. Set up a system of values.

Students can lose money for the following reasons:

$ ___ no pencil

$ ___ no homework

$ ___ chewing gum

$ ___ eating in class

$ ___ running in the hall

Students can earn money for the following reasons:

$ ___ a clean desk

$ ___ a good grade

$ ___ bringing homework

$ ___ being helpful

# Tips for Student Behavior

Payday *(cont.)*

Adjust rules as you wish. Have an end-of-the-period sale. Provide small items that the students can purchase such as stickers, books, pencils, etc., or even a no-homework night.

Rewards at No Cost

If you do not want to always buy things as rewards, here are a few reward ideas that do not cost anything.

- ✓ be first in line
- ✓ draw on the board
- ✓ use the computer
- ✓ no-homework-night pass
- ✓ go to the library
- ✓ be the teacher helper
- ✓ do work at the teacher's desk
- ✓ move desk to another place
- ✓ read to a younger class or student
- ✓ have extra center time
- ✓ operate the projector
- ✓ go to another room for lunch

Zip the Lips

Make a large set of lips, complete with zipper. Cue in your students that when you make a zip motion over the lips, the meaning is the following: "Zip your lips." In other words, get quiet!

Tips for Student Behavior

Fishing on Friday

Want to have good behavior during the week? One way to encourage following rules is to have a special surprise. Obtain two small fish bowls. Label the bowls, one bowl for the girls and one bowl for the boys. At the end of the week, have a drawing for both the boys and girls. Place the students' names in the appropriate bowl if a student was good for the week and followed all the rules. Have some type of special treat for the week's winner.

Smile Face Reminder

Sometimes it is hard to remember to smile. Make a large smiley face and suspend it from the ceiling. When you notice it, it will be a great reminder to stay positive.

Be Human

Students need to know that teachers are human, too. Everyone makes mistakes, even the teacher. Sometimes it is effective to deliberately make a mistake in order to let the students react and correct! When using this approach, be careful that you do not let students get away with being disrespectful. Students respect is a necessary component of good teaching.

Silent Signals and Signs

Silent signaling to your class is always a plus. To silently signal to students that they should stop talking, create a signal light. Put up the red signal when they are too noisy and need to be quiet. Put up the yellow signal when they can talk and share in low voices. Use the green signal for saying talking is all right. If money is no problem, purchase a small stoplight through a teacher supply company.

Other proven methods involve using hand signals. A thumbs up can mean "excellent" or "I'm proud of you." Work with your students to develop signs. This can be a fun way to talk about people who are deaf and how they communicate with each other.

Tips
for
Reading

Tips for Reading

ABC Order

At most home-building stores, you can find simple, countertop materials. Ask to obtain twenty-six samples of color rectangles, one for each letter of the alphabet. Most countertop samples have holes predrilled in the tops. Using a permanent marker, write one letter of the alphabet on each sample. You can use these samples for sequencing the ABCs. Find a place in the classroom where you can put Velcro dots for a special work area. Place Velcro dots on back of the samples. This can be an independent project or a small group project. (*Note:* You can use the same idea for teaching of dictionary skills. You can sequence words in alphabetical order.)

A-B-C Bags

Obtain a box of inexpensive white garbage bags, containing at least twenty-six bags. Cut a slit in the closed portion of each bag for a head hole. Cut arm slots. With a permanent magic marker, write one letter of the alphabet on each bag. Then, play an alphabet game line-up. Have students draw a garbage bag from a box or paper bag. Let each student put on his or her garbage bag as a jacket. On cue, students line up in correct alphabet sequence.

Match-Up Alphabet

Take a different avenue to encourage younger students to learn the sequence of the letters of the alphabet. Use beans! (*Note:* Large dried lima beans work well.) Using a permanent marker, write a single letter of the alphabet on each bean. Spray with acrylic spray for durability. Do as many sets of letters as you wish. Store sets in small plastic zipper bags. Then store in a shoebox decorated and labeled as sequencing materials.

An alternative to this idea is to have a butter bean race. Divide students into small groups. Have them race to see which team can line up the A-B-Cs first!

Another idea is to use elbow macaroni instead of butter beans. Write the letters of the alphabet on the macaroni. Obtain durable cord and string the macaroni in A-B-C order. (*Note:* Be sure to make a large knot on one end of the cord—large enough so that the macaroni will not slip off.)

f Letters

make a division line with masking tape to divide the room into two areas, a first half and a second half. The teacher will be the letter *M*. The teacher will stand in the middle, dividing the room in half. Let each student draw a letter of the alphabet from a stack of prepared cards. As each student draws a card, he or she will each go to where that letter would be located. Is the letter at the first half of the alphabet or the second half?

Sequencing Sentences

Try this idea. Make up sentences by writing one word each on several index cards. Or use a sentence strip and cut apart the words. Divide the class into groups and have them stand in front getting in order of the sentence structure. This skill can be increased, with learning, to more difficult sentences.

| Tim | ran | to | the | park | • |

Magazine Sequencing

Bring a collection of old magazines to school. Have students work in groups to find objects or words that begin with each letter of the alphabet. Allow each group to make a book showing their findings.

Comic Sequencing

For older students, use comic strips for sequencing. Cut out each comic strip, paste to cardboard, and laminate. Then cut apart the strip and file in a plastic zipper bag. Be sure to mix the strips. You may want to put a clue on the back of a single cartoon strip, such as numbering or using alphabet letters.

Soup Can Sequencing

Here is one way to make learning alphabetization different. Save different soup can labels. Cut the labels to size and paste on index cards. Laminate. Students can read and alphabetically sequence the soup label names.

Tips for Reading

Months in Order

Go to a craft store and buy a dozen plastic eggs. On each egg, write a month of the year. Then bring an egg carton from home and number the bottom inside of each egg cup, one to twelve. Students then line up the months, in order, beginning with the first month, January. Make at least two sets and students can have fun pairing together for a "monthly race."

Magnetic Cookie Sheets

Did you ever consider that most cookie sheets are made of a magnetic metal? Use these sheets for magnetic-backed plastic letters and numbers. Students can use the sheets for alphabetizing words, learning to spell words, writing addresses, learning their telephone numbers, etc. Teachers can also use a cookie sheet to stick on notes as reminders. For example: Do not forget the test tomorrow; Remember to have your paper signed; It has been a good day.

Another idea is to paint the cookie sheet with chalkboard paint. Students can write answers to questions or do work on their boards.

Fact or Fiction

Play a game with your students to help them understand fact or fiction.

1. Divide the class into small groups with a captain for each group.

2. Discuss with the students the meaning of fact and fiction.

3. Tell them that a student will stand up and make a statement. The statement may be a fact or it might be fiction and made up.

4. As a group, the students will have to decide. The captain will tell the teacher its decision.

Keep score. It is a fun game with a good learning experience. You can also change it by having the teacher make statements. Use the same group format and have fun! Not only are you teaching about fact and fiction, you are also teaching cooperation.

Braille Alphabet

Do not forget the Braille alphabet when you are discussing the different ways that people learn to read. Students will have fun using the Braille alphabet to write simple words, notes, or sentences. Students can write spelling words using this alphabet. It is a fun way to reinforce how to spell words, as students will unconsciously reinforce the words as they look up the Braille symbols. This is a real challenge for the child who is bored all the time.

Classroom Newspaper

Consider having a classroom newspaper for parent information. Students enjoy creating and developing submissions to be included in the newspaper, and the parents enjoy knowing what is going on. This makes for excellent parent rapport.

Following Directions

There are also many low cost recipes to encourage students to read directions. Think about getting parents involved in sending ingredients and ideas. A recipe is a great topic for inclusion in a class newspaper. Use the sample peanut butter recipe below to start. Not only do you end up with a recipe where you follow directions, you are also teaching how to measure liquids.

Peanut Butter

Materials

✓ 1 1/2 tablespoons of vegetable oil   ✓ 1/2 teaspoon of salt

✓ cup of unsalted roasted peanuts   ✓ blender

Directions

1. Have students measure all of the amounts.

2. Put all ingredients into a blender.

Tips for Reading

"Stump You" Questions

Have a weekly "Stump You" question for the class. Set the last day of the week for answers to be turned in. Allow the students to use resources as they wish. You may make suggestions to the students on where to find answers to questions such as books, encyclopedias, libraries, parents, relatives, etc. Keep a "Stump You" chart of all students in the room. If they find the correct answer, place a check mark or sticker by their name. See who can find the most answers in a set time period. Offer rewards for the diligence of each student. Your rewards could be special privileges—a token prize such as a special pencil or a no-homework night. Post a question on the board relative to the age group you are teaching.

Some examples for kindergarten through first grade are as follows:

- ✓ How many things are in a dozen?
- ✓ Who was our first President?
- ✓ How many inches are in one foot?

Some examples for second and third grades are as follows:

- ✓ What is petrified rock?
- ✓ What is the equator?
- ✓ Who invented the first telephone?

Some examples for upper grades are as follows:

- ✓ How fast can an ostrich run?
- ✓ What is a meteorite?
- ✓ Can you name the planets in order?
- ✓ Can you name the colors of the rainbow?

You can also incorporate interviewing into this challenge. If you plan on having students interviewing teachers, make sure that you have communicated and obtained permission from that teacher, as well as the principal. Have them research answers to questions such as the following:

- ✓ What is the principal's middle name?
- ✓ What college did Mr. Jones graduate from?
- ✓ How many people are on the staff at this school?
- ✓ Can you put their names in alphabetical order?

Tips for Reading

A Special Place

For a great place to read or simply for decoration in your room, try this idea. Make a tree. Students can sit under the tree for reading or for other quiet work. Go to a carpet store and ask them to save, for your class, the heavy cardboard roll on which the carpet is stored. This becomes the trunk of your tree. You will need to cut it somewhat to make it shorter. Secure it uprightly, safely, and solidly in a bucket with plaster of Paris. Next, find an old umbrella with a straight support and handle. You will place this in the top of the carpet roll. Cover the umbrella with large green leaves to make a tree.

Reading Record Box

Take a box and cover it with brightly-colored contact paper. Label the box Reading Record Box. After duplicating student reading record sheets, paste the sheets to some type of backing, such as construction paper, for durability. These sheets are used to record the stories that each student has read. Place each student reading record sheet in alphabetical order by first name only. Make it a rule that each student returns the sheets in the same ABC order he or she pulled it from. Not only will the students read and report, they get practice using ABC order when they return their sheets to the box.

When a student reads a story or a book, have the student give you a report on the story or book. If the student can successfully tell about the book, allow the student to get his or her own reading record sheet from the Reading Record Box. The teacher can date and initial the paper.

"Popcorn" Reading

Sometimes, when doing group reading, not everyone is paying attention. A fun way to keep students alert during oral reading is to call out the word, "popcorn." The student who is reading stops and the next student must pick up in the exact spot. The students will enjoy the challenge, and you will have all students paying attention.

Tips for Reading

Cereal Boxes

Have you ever thought about using cereal boxes for reading? You can find a wealth of information on these boxes. Cut out the front box cover and the side ingredients. Make a copy of these. Then put the two copies together, front and back. Form your question sheet and work with your students.

Stories on Tape

In all classes there are usually several students who are below grade level. Record the story to be read on tape. Any student who wishes to read and follow along with the tape can do so. Set up an area where the tape recorder and earphones are kept for student use.

Special Reading Corner

Why not have a special reading corner where students can read at leisure when finished with their work? One easy way to make it attractive is by doing the following:

1. Obtain several football jerseys. (Yard sales yield many good buys.)

2. Sew the sleeve ends and the neck closed.

3. Stuff the jerseys with poly-batting and close the opening at the bottom.

4. Stack your jerseys in a corner for a relaxing reading time.

Divide Them Up

Syllabication is a necessary skill that students need to learn. Here is a different approach to teaching that skill. To introduce words, make a pull tab type of holder, as shown, for strips to be pulled through:

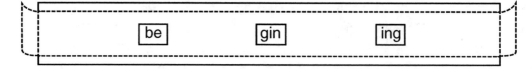

be   gin   ing

Cut out windows in the holder. On a separate piece of poster board or heavy paper, divide a word into syllables. Have the student pull the strip to the windows. The word will show in the windows and will give the students a visual way to look at syllabication. Once your holders are complete, making the pull strips is an easy task.

50

Tips for Reading

Visual Cues

If you have trouble with students reading instructions on how to do something, place a visual cue around each word on the board or on the worksheet. For a sentence that needs a capital, write capitalize in bold letters. For things that need circling, write the word circle and draw a circle around it. For things that need underlining, write the word underline with a line drawn under it. Such visual cues will draw attention to your directions. Another good idea for understanding directions is to have the directions read by the teacher. Have the students reinforce the words by circling or underlining and then repeat verbally what they are to do.

Dictionary Guide Words

How do you go about making guide words become an active part of a student's learning? Make students active in learning about guide words through the activity below.

1. Choose two students to stand up and be the "Guides."

2. Hand out the cards with words that would be between the two "Guides." Write them large enough for all the class to see.

3. On cue, have students line up in the alphabetical order that would be found between the two "Guides."

(*Note:* Begin by using only three to four words between the two "Guides." As the students begin to understand, increase the number of words.)

Menu Reading

Menus offer much in the way of reading. You can ask a variety of questions such as the costs of various meals. You can also learn new vocabulary words such as the examples below:

✓ appetizers	✓ baked	✓ casserole
✓ entrees	✓ soufflé	✓ marinated
✓ gratuity	✓ braised	✓ broiled

You can also have students use the menu to order a meal, staying as close to a given cost as possible.

Tips for Reading

Magazine Subscription Stamps

Where do you put all of those magazine advertisements that come in the mail requiring you to paste the magazine stickers on the card to send back? Put these ads to good use in the classroom by saving the magazine stamps. Use them to teach reading for information. Paste several on a sheet of paper, place a number by each one, and then ask the following questions:

✓ What is the name of this magazine?

✓ How many issues are in the subscription?

✓ What is the price per issue of this subscription?

✓ How much is the total cost? (Students need to understand when there are 3 payments of $2.56 each, you have to either add or multiply to obtain the answer.)

✓ How many installments will I have to pay if I order?

✓ What is each installment price?

✓ Are there any free gifts with this subscription?

✓ Looking at all three magazines, which is the least expensive?

✓ Which is more expensive?

See how many questions you can get from just these ads. When you have developed the worksheet for students to use, copy it in your files for future reference. Consider pasting one magazine advertisement per sheet of paper. Have students answer the questions about just one magazine ad instead of two or three. Set up a few challenges in one of the learning centers. You can laminate the ads and keep them for use over and over.

Key Word of the Day

Have a daily learning experience by having new words for the students to learn. Give a bonus point for the first student to find the definition in the dictionary. Post your key word in a prominent place in your classroom. Then, at random times during the day, call on a student to give the meaning of the key word of the day. Give a bonus point to the student. (*Note:* To be fair, you will have to use a check sheet to make sure you reach all of the students.)

Fishing for Sounds

Need something to stimulate learning letter sounds? You will need a fish stencil, scissors, heavy construction paper or poster board, felt tip markers, paper clips, a magnet, string, and a yardstick for a pole. Trace and cut out several fish. Decorate each fish and attach a metal paper clip to each fish. On each fish, write a sound. Attach string to magnet and the string to the pole. You now have a fishing pole. Students can fish for sounds, make the letter sounds, and tell words that begin with the sound. You can also change the fishing for sounds to fishing for addition problems or subtraction problems. Use your imagination.

Put It Right

Make a simple poster with the sounds you are studying as shown in the following example:

short a	long a
tap	tape
cap	cape

Write words you are studying on cardboard and attach a piece of tape to the back. Have students determine which sound the word will go under—the short a or the long a column. This is a good way to introduce the silent "e" rule using a visual and an auditory medium.

Catalog Order Form

Use a catalog order form to figure prices and to find information. You can easily cut and paste ads for use by the students. Give each student a copy with his or her order form. Some examples of questions that can be asked are as follows:

✓ How much does the item cost?

✓ In what sizes does the item come?

✓ What colors are offered?

✓ What is your total price of your order?

✓ Do you have to pay tax?

✓ How is your order sent?

✓ What is the catalog number?

✓ How much does the item weigh?

Tips
for
Language

Tips for Language

Window Shades

It is worth your money to go out and purchase several inexpensive window shades. These can be used for displaying examples or cues for directional activities. You can easily attach the shade to a board by adding monofilament line or a cord. When finished with the display, just roll up the shade. It is easy to store. You may want to spray it with a clear acrylic spray or cover it with contact paper. Hang a shade to display the following:

✓ how to write friendly letters (showing placement for heading, greeting, body, closing, and signature)

✓ how to address envelopes

Vocabulary Illustrations

Make vocabulary learning fun by giving students a list of words that can be illustrated. For example, if the word scared is selected, make shaky letters as shown:

scared

Have students illustrate some of the words below. Let the students use their imaginations.

✓ sweet	✓ sour	✓ run
✓ sit	✓ hot	✓ cold
✓ steamy	✓ love	✓ tired
✓ sad	✓ fiery	✓ smoky

Mate Search

If you want to teach synonyms, write a synonym and the "synonym mate" separately on halved index cards. Do enough to pass out to each student. On cue, students search for their "synonym mate." If you are working on learning vocabulary words, write the vocabulary word on one card and a short definition on another. Students search for their "vocabulary mate."

Tips for Language

Puzzle Pieces

For younger children, make puzzle parts for synonyms or antonyms. Make puzzle pieces out of poster board and laminate. You can make more than one set easily and put these in your learning center for use at any time. This same technique works wonderfully well for teaching history facts, science facts, studying for exams.

Contraction Search

When teaching contractions, try using magazines or sheets of newspaper. Have students search for words that are contractions. Give each student a highlighter to use or share in a small group. Set a time limit to see how many can be found, either individually or in a small group. It is a good way to focus attention on contractions.

Color Association

Every teacher needs to teach students how to write stories with creative words. Expand students' awareness of their environment by thinking of describing words. Using colors is one way to talk about adjectives as words describing things. Write the following colors on the board: red, blue, black, brown, white, yellow, green, and purple. Ask the students to think of describing words that would be associated with the colors. Look at the examples below.

- ✓ red—blushing, flashy, shiny, bright
- ✓ white—snowy, icy, pure, plain
- ✓ black—scary, dark, empty, dismal, dreary

You can use this same technique in naming nouns that are associated with the color words.

- ✓ red—strawberries, lips, apples, or peppermint candy
- ✓ blue—sky, birds, or water
- ✓ white—bride, vase, snow, clouds, or cotton
- ✓ green—grass, leaves, cucumber, or a pickle

Tips for Language

Magazine Search

Use those old magazines for a terrific group, school, or home project. Save them for special lessons. For example, have students locate the following:

✓ common nouns, proper nouns

✓ descriptive words or pictures

✓ action words or pictures

✓ categories of words such as people words, sales words, emotional words

Pantomime Time

In order to reinforce the difference between a noun and verb, have a time to pantomime. Have a student draw a slip of paper with the word written on it. Then, have the student act out the word. At first, only introduce nouns. Pantomime nouns relating to animals, people, occupations, and objects. Next, introduce verbs by pantomiming emotions and actions. After the students become familiar with the game and understand it, add adjectives. Some examples of adjectives include pantomiming an angry man, a crying girl, or a happy person.

Interjections and Exclamation Marks

Teach through acting out the word to keep students' attention. Take poster board and draw a funny character face. Attach a magnetic strip to the face and place it on the magnetic board. Write interjections on poster board and attach a magnetic strip. As you say each word, pop the word on the board. Talk about emphasis and how it affects words we say. Words you can use include the following:

✓ wow   ✓ great   ✓ gee   ✓ boo

✓ gosh   ✓ terrific   ✓ yea   ✓ ouch

It is also interesting to demonstrate how just the tone of voice can change meaning.

Tips for Language

Word Webbing

Word webbing has been around for a long time, but have you tried it with your students? It is an excellent way to increase vocabulary and thinking skills. For example, write the word, *lady*. Then ask students to suggest related words, drawing lines from the word, *lady*, to the descriptive words.

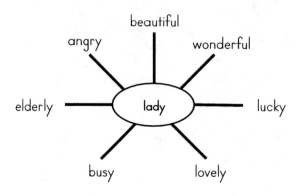

Word Volleyball

When working with synonyms or antonyms, play Word Volleyball. Divide students into teams. For example, let us say the class is working on synonyms. The first person in line draws a word from prepared game cards. That student reads the word aloud and the first student on the opposite side must give a synonym. The game continues, bouncing a word back and forth until someone cannot give an answer. The last team to give a correct answer wins the point.

You can use the game to name descriptive adjectives or to name as many things in one category as possible. Some examples include the following: things that you ride, kinds of vegetables or fruits, different occupations, or kinds of sports. The game is very versatile and the students love this type of interaction.

Tips for Language

Word Association Game

Here is a time-filler game that is fun and stimulates associative thinking. Make up a list of things associated with each other. Ask students to tell how these words are alike or what they have in common. The number of categories you use is unlimited and only dependent on the learning levels of your students.

Some examples of words include the following:

- ✓ coat, mittens, cap, boots (winter wear; all clothing)
- ✓ apple, pear, plum, lemon (types of fruits)
- ✓ spring, summer, fall, winter (seasons)
- ✓ thunder, snow, lightning, rain (kinds of weather)
- ✓ elf, sleigh, gifts, reindeer (things about Christmas)

Some examples of categories include the following:

✓ occupations	✓ types of clocks
✓ types of mail	✓ Halloween words (or another holiday)
✓ kinds of dogs	✓ summer activities
✓ subject areas	✓ things we read
✓ things we ride	✓ things that are nouns

Oddball Word Association Game

Here is another listing game for students to use associative thinking skills. Call out a list of words, asking which word does not belong. Some examples are stated below.

- ✓ boots, socks, slippers, galoshes, gloves (*gloves: all others you wear on your feet*)
- ✓ puppy, kitten, calf, goat, colt (*goat: all others name baby animals*)
- ✓ bedroom, door, den, kitchen, garage (*door: all others are room areas in the home*)
- ✓ truck, train, canoe, scooter, car (*canoe: all others travel on land*)

This list is endless. You can think of so many categories to name. Just be sure that you put the oddball word in different spots in your list.

Tips for Language

Compound Word Eggs

Here is an idea that could easily be used in a center or a group activity area. Draw eggs large enough for compound words to be written on halves.

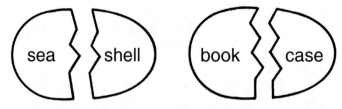

Students can work together, or individually, to match pieces so as to have a compound word for each egg. Storing them in plastic, zipper bags would be one way of safely keeping the activity.

Another way to present this activity would be to make and laminate an activity folder. On the back of the folder, secure an envelope to hold the compound parts. Students are able to take the parts and arrange them into compound words. Should you wish to have this as a graded activity, it is suggested that you use Velcro on the folder and the compound parts.

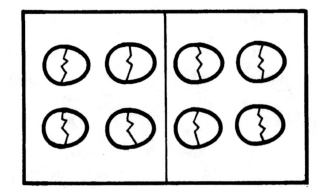

Plethora of Prepositions

For a fun activity to teach prepositions, divide the class into teams and see which team can come up with the most prepositions. For a creative touch, have the students write the prepositions in a whirl pattern, using different colored pencils.

Tips for Language

Double or Nothing Compound Words

Students can exercise with these compound words. Double the fun with this activity. Students must identify a word that will make the top word and the bottom word into two different compound words.

jelly
fish
net

What word can you add to make these words into a compound word?

The answer is fish. You can have a jellyfish and a fishnet.

Other words that can be combined are as follows:

✓ work (book) case   ✓ bed (room) mate

✓ out (side) walk   ✓ sun (light) house

✓ snow (ball) game   ✓ life (time) out

✓ with (out) side   ✓ under (water) way

(*Note:* This may be difficult for some students if you do not list the compound words on the board or on a sheet. It all depends on the learning style of the student.)

Compound Word Match

Make up a list of words where students have to match words to form compounds. Some examples include the following:

✓ _____room (bed, bath)

✓ _____ball (foot, base, soft)

✓ _____light (sun, moon)

✓ star_____ (light, fish, ship)

✓ silver_____ (ware, fish)

✓ out_____ (side, doors, field)

✓ _____ground (under, back)

✓ back_____ (ground, log, board, pack)

Tips for Language

Compound Word Art

You can also challenge students to make "compound word art." They will draw pictures. For example, you can use the compound word *rainbow*. On their papers, they would draw a picture of rain, put a plus mark, and then draw a picture of a bow. In other words, *rain* + *bow* gives you one word—*rainbow*.

Example:

rain   +   bow   star   +   fish

Be sure that you talk about each compound word and ask questions to ensure understanding.

Compound Go Fishing

Use the old game of "Go Fish" to work on compound words. Blank cards can be readily obtained at teacher supply stores. Make several sets. Four or five students can be grouped to play the game. Half of the cards will have one-half of a compound word written on them. Students will have to "fish" for completion of the compound word. Do not to make the compound words too difficult for lower level elementary students. They should be words that would be common to them. Lists of various compound words can be written on the board or on laminated sheets for each student.

Punctuation Action

When working with students on punctuation, try this technique. After writing a sentence on the board, use a cue for the ending. For example:

- ✓ using a period—stomp one time
- ✓ using a comma—utter a "hum-m-m-m" sound
- ✓ using a question—raise your hand as if to ask
- ✓ using an exclamation mark—utter "oh" loudly

Then, read a sentence and have the students call out the correct ending punctuation using the actions given. Be careful not to let your students get too loud!

Dead Words

Prior to beginning this assignment, tape the following dialogue:

> "Good morning, agents. You are about to be assigned a very important mission. It is important that you bury all of the 'dead' words. No one else can be responsible. There are people who use one word over and over again. This is boring and dangerous. Readers lose interest. These words must be eliminated. Your mission is to replace these five words: said, happy, pretty, good, and bad. Put each word at the top page. You must find words that can take their place. Now, detectives, you can take the word, *said*. Think of what words you might use in the place of this word. Write them on your list.

> You must follow through with your mission. Everyone is counting on you. In ten seconds, this message will destroy. Good luck, agents! Get busy on your mission."

Assign students to groups of four or five. Hand each group sheets with the five overused words. Play the tape recording. Allow ample time for brainstorming. Have dictionaries and thesauruses available for each group to use.

Complete your activity by designing a bulletin board with tombstones, complete with the letters R.I.P. (rest in peace). After the students have completed their assignments, write new words on strips to be placed on the board. Students will have a feeling of accomplishment and also a cue to new words to use when writing.

Tips for Language

Observable Opposites

For the younger students, use observable items to develop concepts when possible. For example, if you were to talk about light vs. heavy, collect items for students to test and chart. Examples include the following: feathers, cotton balls, a pencil, a leaf, a book. It is an endless list. After trying to see if something is light enough for students to blow away, have them chart their answers on the board.

Light	Heavy

Use the same type of activity with sweet vs. sour, full vs. empty, happy vs. sad. You will find more opposites that you can use.

Stirring Up Adjectives

Here is a cute way to teach adjectives. Remind students that adjectives are words that describe. On poster board, draw a cooking pot. On the pot, label with a wide-tip marker, "Adjective Pot." Place magnets on the back of the pot and attach it to the board for your lesson. Have students call out words that describe. Write these words on the board as though they are coming out of the pot. After brainstorming with the students, take each word and call on a student to make a sentence using one of the "pot" words. You can use the same activity for overused words (i.e., said, pretty), for adverbs, interrogative words, or words of exclamation.

Tips
for
Writing

Tips for Writing

Which Side of the Paper?

You may have a student or two who do not know where to start on a paper or in which directions they need to work. They may begin on the wrong side or complete the work up-side-down. Think about teaching the phrase "'hole' your left thumb out." Holes are on the left. A flat hand with the thumbs extended outward teaches the left thumb points to the "hole" side.

Stringing Cereal

When working with small children on motor coordination skills for writing, try this idea. It is easy and yummy. Use some type of round-shaped cereal. Have students string the pieces using string or yarn. They then can eat the pieces off the string.

Trace Me

Make letter formation cards by tracing over alphabet letters with a thin stream of school glue. Students can trace over the letters to learn the alphabet. This tactile method is also useful in learning to write one's name.

Tile Letters

For those children needing to learn their lower case letters, have them play an alphabet-matching game. Use the small tiles that you can get from homebuilding stores and write the upper and lower case letters on them. Students will match the lower case letters to the upper case letters as a learning center activity.

Brown Bag It

To get students into creative writing, why don't you "brown bag it"? Get a large grocery bag. Fill it with items that a story could be written about, such as the following: a travel brochure, a set of keys, a silk flower, a microphone, a camera, a blank diary, and so forth. Have one item for each student. Have each student reach into the bag and pull out an item. This is to be his or her story starter.

Design a Product

For a writing assignment, have the students design some type of product and make the advertisements for the product. For example, one student may make a new type of perfume or a racing car. No two students should have the same idea.

Invent Me

For creative writing, perpetuate ideas for students to invent. Take a basket and have a certain need written on strips of paper. Here are some examples:

✓ Your pet needs a way to ride with you on a bicycle. Design a way for your pet to enjoy bicycling.

✓ You do not like to clean your room. Invent a way to keep your room clean.

✓ Invent a new toy with wings.

✓ Invent a car that does not need a driver. How will the car know where to go?

Sentence Expansion

In beginning writing, students seem to use very simple sentences. Encourage expansion of sentences by doing this activity. When beginning, read aloud a simple sentence like the one below.

Example: The man fell.

Then ask the students to contribute thoughts such as the examples below.

✓ "Where did the man fall?"

✓ "In what other places could this man fall?"

✓ "What is the age of the man?"

✓ "What different words can we use to describe this man?"

Add their details to the sentence as shown in the example below.

Example: The elderly man fell on the soft ground.

Tips for Writing

What a Yarn

You can have a "ball" stringing with this idea. You will only need two things: a ball of yarn and students who will listen.

Instruct all the students to sit in a circle on the floor. Tell them that they are going to have to listen carefully and make up a story. Each student will have a part in creating this story. Hand a ball of yarn to one student. This student is the story starter. The student will begin a story with a single sentence. The first student holds the end of the yarn and rolls the ball of yarn to another student. The second student will tell the next sentence of the story. Again, this students holds a part of the yarn, and passes the ball of yarn to the next student until all students have contributed to the story. Tape-record their story and play it back to the students. You will have laughter galore at the story they have created.

Fostering Creativity

Develop a creative writing activity with these topic suggestions on nursery rhyme and fairy tale characters:

- ✓ How Humpty Dumpty became one of the king's men
- ✓ How the three little pigs turned the table on the wolf
- ✓ How Little Miss Muffet trained her spider
- ✓ Why Snow White wasn't welcomed by the dwarfs
- ✓ How Cinderella became a fairy godmother

Class Newspaper

Have students participate in a class newspaper. Vote to choose an editor and have as many reporters as you wish. The reporters will need guidance on the types of questions to ask. This can easily be done in small-group instruction.

Have a special reporter to gather news from the office of the principal. Have another reporter interview a particular teacher or the school custodian. Have one student responsible for finding appropriate jokes or making a comic strip for the newspaper. Have a question box so students can put in a question without anyone knowing who asked the question. Then have someone publish the question and answer in the newspaper.

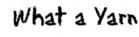

Tips for Writing

Weekly Writing

Try some of these ideas for writing during the week. Write three questions on the board before students arrive. Tell them that they must answer all the questions in complete sentences. Remind them to use their best handwriting. Alter the activities on each day. See the examples below for ideas.

Monday Mumbo—On Monday questions should center around the weekend—places the student might have gone, a special event that happened, a kindness act the student saw or did, etc.

Tuesday Trivia—Tuesday's questions could be questions on what a certain vocabulary word might mean, an idiom or simile meaning to define, an off-beat question, etc.

Wednesday Work—Wednesday's work might be simply to look up meanings of assigned words or a letter to a business or person asking for a particular job and telling why he or she would be the best one for the job.

Thursday Theater—Thursday's Theater work might be a script to be read by two people. It might be a simple creative thought or a list of actions for playing charades.

Friday's Funnies—Friday's Funnies might be jokes or stories of funny things that are either made-up or real incidents.

Whatever you do, make it interesting and a light challenge for each student. Give a set amount of time. At first, you will not get much from the students, but as days and weeks progress, you will see improvement in their writing.

Terrible Bs and Ds

Teaching the differences between a "b" and a "d" can give small children difficulty. Here is a well-used technique that works!

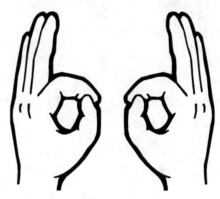

Hold your hands in front of you. Point the four fingers upward. Take the index finger and the thumb on each hand and form a circle. The left hand should look like a "b" and the right should look like a "d."

Tips for Writing

Life Timeline

Have each student make a scroll timeline of his or her life. Suggested times students might include in the timeline are as follows: when they began school, birth, birth of siblings, when they first played sports on a team, any time they moved from one place to another, any special trip, etc.

Antonyms

Combine writing with a specific language skill. Write several paragraphs containing antonyms. Underline all antonyms. Have students rewrite the paragraphs using the opposites of the underlined words.

To introduce younger children to the concept of an antonym, have them listen to a specific direction, such as: "Everyone cry." Tell the students to do the opposite of what was asked. The teacher would reinforce that opposite words are called antonyms. Some other "opposite" examples to use are as follows:

- ✓ "Look left."
- ✓ "Pull your left ear."
- ✓ "Stand."
- ✓ "Nod no."
- ✓ "Wave your right hand."
- ✓ "Touch your toes."

Pretending Time

A time for pretending can be great for creative writing. Take an old pair of shoes and paint the shoes red. Add glitter and other decorations. Challenge the students to write about "Where their special shoes" take them.

Invisible Ink

Making invisible ink is not difficult. You will need lemon juice, white paper, and a cotton swab or small brush. Instruct students to write lightly as a little invisible ink will go a long way. Too much and the paper will buckle and the writing will show.

To read the invisible secret message, carefully hold the paper over heat. Be careful not to let the paper catch fire!

Mail Time!

In a special part of your room, set up a brightly painted mailbox. It can be set on a table or you can make a stand. Students love to write notes. Explain to your students that this mailbox is everyone to receive and send mail. Every week or two, select a mail person. During the initial morning activities while attendance and other duties are taking place, the mailman can deliver mail. The teacher can have special letters to students to commend them for good work, or just to say, "you're special" or to answer a student's letter. Students can write letters to the teacher. Remind the students that mail will only be delivered at certain times of the day and that writing letters will take place only during certain times. Set the rules initially.

Anther good use for a mailbox is to have students put in any notes from parents or excuses when they first come inside in the morning. Your mail person will deliver all mail at the set time. This affords a way to keep all correspondence from parents together. Sometimes a teacher's desk can become just too cluttered and inadvertently correspondence can get lost in the shuffle.

Envelopes should be no problem. Just save all those junk mail envelopes and cover the front for addressing. Many of the card companies at the end of a holiday or other special time of celebration, keep only the cards and discard the envelopes. Visit a store to ask for these envelopes or contact the card store supplier to find the date of the next restocking.

What Did You Wish?

For creative early morning writing, give students three wishes. You can organize the wishes into parts: Your first wish is a wish that you can go some place. Tell why you want to go to the place you name. Your second wish is to wish for something you do not have. Tell why you want it. Your third wish is a wish about what you want to do when you grow up. Tell why you want to do this.

Tips for Writing

Alphabetical Order

Have students list names of all students in the room and order these words in alphabetical order, listing last names first. Give examples so that they see that a comma is necessary. Here is another idea for alphabetical order. In most schools, copies of the school handbooks are usually kept in the classroom for teacher use. The faculty is listed. Have students put faculty names in alphabetical order.

Writing Time Fillers

Every teacher needs time fillers. When the teacher is conducting early morning required activities, always have something for students to do. These ideas need to be varied and ones that can keep students' attention.

Brainstorming Adjectives: If the class is working on learning about adjectives, write a noun on the board and challenge students to see who can come up with the most adjectives describing the word. Allow students to get in small groups, if they wish.

My Word: Write a word on the board that relates to a certain celebration and have students see how many words can be made of this one word. Many holidays or special times of the year can foster this activity. Try these special days: Halloween, Thanksgiving, Christmas, Hanukkah, Kawanzaa, Columbus Day, President's Day, Valentine's Day, Labor Day, Mother's Day.

Dictionary Skills: List words that are new to students. Have thesauruses and dictionaries readily available. Students look up the new words and try to make a sentence with the new word, or words. You might also have students look up specific words to determine from what language the word originally came. Or have students look up specific words to determine what is the part of speech.

Telephone Book Search: Have students look up various businesses in telephone books and record them on paper. In this case, you would have to have enough books for all students. Some examples include the following: plumber, lumber yard, barber shop, or trucking company. Giving the students this challenge can be carried over into additional lessons on informational searches.

Tips
for
Spelling

Tips for Spelling

Star Bulletin Board

For weekly tests, have a special spelling bulletin board. Title it, "Spelling Stars Are Out of This World." For each student who makes an A on the test, put his or her name on a cutout star on the bulletin board.

One quick way to make this idea easier is to make your stars ahead of time and put the name of a student on each star and laminate them. This way, you are ready to put up your spelling stars within minutes of grading the tests!

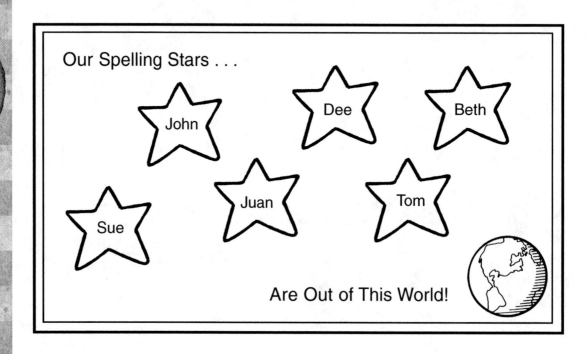

Some other caption ideas are as follows:

✓ Top Stars
✓ Reach for the Stars
✓ Check Out Our Spelling Stars

✓ Star Spellers
✓ Stars of the Week
✓ Stars Above

Tips for Spelling

A Star-Filled Room

Why not make hanging mobiles? You can attach names of students who make a high grade on stars for a "star-filled" room. The stars can be very motivational. You might even want to add an end-of-the-semester bonus prize for the student who has the most stars. If your students are divided into levels of spelling, award a bonus prize for each group. Be sure to note individual differences and make sure that the challenge is within reach of all.

"Sick Words"

Using a bulletin board or wall space, design a hospital sick ward with the following materials:

✓ large unlined index cards   ✓ craft sticks

✓ permanent marker   ✓ stapler

Then follow the directions below.

1. Use index cards to cut a simple bed shape. For bulletin board use, staple sides and bottom to board. Leave top open. For wall space, you will have to use two cards in order to make a "bed pocket."

2. You will need enough space to put each student's "sick bed" on the bulletin board or the wall.

3. Label each student's "bed."

4. When you have the pre-test, missed words go on a wooden craft stick. These are the "sick words." When students are studying for their final tests, they can put extra effort into studying their "sick words." This is a good time to pair the student who is having difficulty with another student who is more advanced. On test day, they get to take their "sick words" that they correctly spelled out of the hospital.

Tips for Spelling

Spelling in Braille

This project will take a little more time and is for upper elementary students. Make copies of a printed Braille system. Then, ask the students to write their words using the Braille alphabet. In order to accomplish this, they will have to concentrate on the letters and the way the word is spelled. It is just a fun way to remember how to spell a particular word.

Spelling with Sign Language

All students are fascinated with sign language. Why not use this fascination in spelling? Teach the students how to finger spell. Then, have a spelling bee where the students have to stand up in front of the class and spell a word in sign language. You are using a great multi-sensory approach in learning! To practice for the spelling bee, have students pair together to work on how to spell each word. First work on spelling the word aloud; next, work on spelling the word in sign language.

Spelling Demons

Keep a list posted of spelling demons, words that are often misspelled. This is helpful in any type of writing activity.

Add Them Up

Develop an ABC chart and assign a numerical value to each letter. For example: A = 1, B = 2, C = 3, and so forth. Then, develop word sheets using the numerical values and have students figure out the words for the week's spelling. Students will take this for fun, yet, they are committing the spelling words to memory just by working on the sheet.

Stories for Spelling

Develop several different paragraphs or stories using the spelling words for the week. In the spelling center, have a list of the week's spelling words for the students' use. Have the students fill out a record stating how many of each spelling word was found in the paragraphs or stories. Again, the students are committing spelling words to memory.

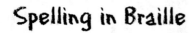

Tips for Spelling

Bong It

Here is a fun game to help students practice their spelling words. Begin by putting all students in the class in a single file line. Have all spelling words written on strips of paper and folded for drawing from a box. The teacher will draw a word and then say the word.

The first student is required to spell the first letter of the word. The second student spells the second letter and so on, until the spelling word is finished. Should a student state the wrong letter of a word, others yell "Bong." That student must sit down. The play continues until only one student is left standing. A special award can be given to the "winner" such as candy or a non-edible treat.

Found It!

This activity may be somewhat difficult for younger children, but certainly a challenge for any gifted, inquiring student. Offer a challenge to any student to find a spelling error in any form of written materials, from magazines and newspapers, to pamphlets and signs.

Spell in Clay

Younger students will definitely like this exposure to their spelling words. Have them use modeling clay to "spell" their words! Students can form the letters from clay or roll out the dough and inscribe the letters with a toothpick.

Glue It

Have a pile of old magazines in your spelling center for learning. Have students look for the letters of each of their spelling words. Then, have the students cut out and glue down the letters in the appropriate spelling order.

Backward Day

Have a backward spelling bee. It makes the student picture the word in his or her head and call out letters, as they should appear written backwards. Add a bit of competition by dividing into teams. This activity can be loads of fun.

Tips for Spelling

Spelling Freedom Day

Most teachers give a spelling pre-test on Wednesday or Thursday and their weekly spelling test on Friday. Why not give those students who have a perfect paper a "spelling freedom" day? These students can help others by practicing spelling words. During that time, when the Friday test is being given, those students can read a favorite book, create a drawing, or work on other assignments.

Class Response Sticks

Every teacher has those students who wait until another student answers a question and says whatever that student says. Here is an idea that works well. Make a response stick for every student using the following materials: poster board, craft sticks, glue, and a black marker.

Follow the directions below to create a response stick for each student.

1. Cut out circles from poster board (about 3 inches in diameter). Cut two circles per student.

2. Label half the circles "yes" and half the circles "no."

3. On each craft stick, glue a "yes" and a "no" circle, back to back on either side of the stick.

To use this technique, the teacher asks a question that can be answered with the word, "yes" or "no." The students must indicate their answers. Sometimes the teacher must prompt students by snapping fingers to indicate the time at which they must respond. If not, slower students will wait to see what others have answered.

Caution students not to answer prior to the snap. You can use this technique for spelling, asking if you have spelled the word correctly or have written the word correctly. Use the response stick for any subject where this type of answer can be an effective learning technique.

Tips for Spelling

Type It Out

Students love to push the buttons when typing. Use this for a spelling study motivator. Have students type each word five or more times when extra time permits.

Write On!

Trace a simple coloring book page and have the students write their spelling words on the coloring book illustration's lines. They will be writing their words over and over to make the picture. If there is no time to make the page, have them write their words, with an overlay, on the picture itself.

Let Me Count the Ways

You can use a plethora of ideas to have fun with spelling. Think about these suggestions for enhancing spelling.

- ✓ writing spelling words in alphabetical order
- ✓ making silly sentences using spelling words
- ✓ using Braille or Morse code to write the words
- ✓ drawing illustrations of the words
- ✓ using a search-and-find puzzle sheet
- ✓ writing each word in a different color
- ✓ writing words and identifying vowels by colors
- ✓ cutting out the words or letters from magazines or newspapers to make the spelling word
- ✓ finding words that rhyme with the spelling words
- ✓ seeing how many small words can be made from each spelling word
- ✓ writing words using a 3-D effect
- ✓ making a crossword puzzle of spelling words.

It is all up to your imagination. The more the students use and play with their words, the more the words will become imprinted into their memory.

Tips
for

Math

Greater Than/Less Than

Some children have difficulty remembering which way the symbol is facing to show greater than or less than.

Tell the students that Leo, the lion, is eating all the larger numbers because he is a big animal and is always hungry. They will love Leo and you will love the learning that transpires! Keep Leo displayed as a symbol reminder until all students have mastered the knowledge.

$$67 > 42$$

Another alternative idea for display and instruction is to use the Pac-Man figure. This will allow for a visual reminder, too.

Tile Counting

Go to a local decorator/paint store. Purchase sheets of small tiles. They cost very little and will make excellent additions to your counting units and your number sequencing units. Use permanent markers to place numerals on the tiles. Cut the sheets into tile pieces. Tiles can be stored in a potato chip container with a lid. This makes for easy storage. Below are some ways you can use the tiles and containers.

Example: Have one or more containers with tile numbers from 0 to 30. Students will remove tiles and place in numerical order.

Example: Have one or more containers with numbers for counting by 2s or 5s or 10s. Students will remove tiles and place in order.

Sequencing with Poker Chips

Poker chips can be a useful resource in sequencing. Make sets for sequencing the alphabet, for sequencing numerical order, for counting by 2s, 5s, 10s, etc. Use permanent markers to label the poker chips and store them in plastic zipper bags. You could also use this idea for sequencing days of the week or months of the year.

Tips for Math

Poker Chip Numbers

Poker chips can help in learning to write larger numbers. Acquire the following materials: poker chips, permanent marker, and plastic zipper bags.

Follow the directions below.

1. Make two sets of numbers 0–9 for each student.

2. Store in a plastic zipper bag.

3. Teacher calls out a number, such as 358.

4. Students use chips to make the number called by the teacher.

5. Teacher can monitor students, then write the number on the board for all to self-check.

(*Caution:* Be careful to call only numbers that students will be able to make with their poker chips. Remember, students will only have packets with two sets of numbers from 0 to 9. For example, you would not want to call out 555, as the students would not have three 5s.)

An Addition Bee

Give a number card (1, 2, 3, 4, 5, 6, 7, 8, or 9) to each player. Line up into two teams. The teacher calls on the first two students, one from each team. These students stand at the front of the room. The teacher will call out a number such as 12. The two students have to find one player whose number combined with his or her number would add up to the number called by the teacher. For example, Student #1 has the number 5. Student #2 has the number 3. The student with the number 5 can tag a student with the number 7 to add to 12. The student with the number 3 has to get a student with number 9 to add to 12. The student that finds the combination first gets a point for his or her team.

This class game will work with subtraction but only with subtracting from single digit numbers, initially. In addition, the maximum number called will be 17 unless more than two students are used to combine the answer.

Subtraction Ruler Tool

Often, you have a student who has a difficult time remembering whether to subtract the "bottom number" from the "top number." Here is a tool that may be helpful.

Instruct the student to tell you what the "top number" and "bottom number" are in the subtraction problem. For example, if you have 5 minus 2, 5 would be the "top number" and 2 would be the "bottom number." Then on the ruler have the student put the pencil point on the 5, the "top number." Have the student move the pencil over two spaces ("bottom number") to the left to find the answer.

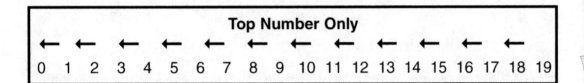

Top Number Only

← ← ← ← ← ← ← ← ← ← ← ←

0 1 2 3 4 5 6 7 8 9 10 11 12 13 14 15 16 17 18 19

This is merely a prelude to borrowing. When the student is ready for borrowing, the subtraction tool will be more effective and useful. Let us say that you have 15 minus 7. Have the student put the pencil point on the 5 (top number). Ask the student to identify the "bottom number," 7. Tell the student to take the 7 from the 5. What happens? The student will find out that there are not enough numbers. So, what must happen? You have to borrow. When you borrow, this number becomes 15. Now, put the pencil point on the "top number," 15. Take 7 from it. It is a visual help. The student sees the problem.

The subtraction ruler tool is not for all students—just for the ones having the most difficulty. It should be used only as a last resort. It is a visual way to see when you must borrow. (*Caution:* You can allow a student having difficulty to learn with it, but you must gradually wean the student off the helper tool.) Be sure to laminate these subtraction rulers, or better yet, make them out of wood and spray with shellac after lettering!

Tips for Math

Number Flip Chart

With this tool, the teacher can flip three numbers and call on a student to read the number. (See picture below for a sample flip chart.) For example, the teacher flips the number strips to 463, and the student will read the number shown. You may wish to assign one student who can read numbers well to work with small groups having difficulty. You can also adapt this idea and make a thousands chart by using additional strips.

Use the following materials to create the flip chart: poster board, hole punch, and three notebook, rings. Then follow the directions below to assemble the flip chart:

1. Using poster board, cut 30 strips approximately 2" x 4".

2. Using hole punch, punch a hole in the top center of each strip.

3. Cut a backing strip, approximately 8" x 6".

4. With three notebook rings, evenly spaced across the top of the backing strip, attach 10 strips on each notebook ring.

5. Number each strip beginning with 0 and going to 9. The first number should be 0. (For durability, you may wish to laminate each strip and the backing.)

Place Value Pockets

Often, place value is difficult for students to grasp. Use a visual for them to hold and use while learning. Call out the number you wish students to show. Students will place the number sticks in the appropriate place value pocket to show the number called. (See illustration below.)

Use the following materials to create this idea for each student: four small coin envelopes, a permanent marker, 8 1/2" x 11" piece of cardstock paper, craft sticks, and a stapler. Then follow the directions below to put together the place value pockets and number sticks:

1. Cut the flaps off the four small coin envelopes.

2. Using a permanent marker, mark each envelope as follows: thousands, hundreds, tens, and ones.

4. Laminate, if desired.

5. Staple envelope pockets onto an 8 1/2" x 11" piece of cardstock paper as shown in the picture.

6. Mark the comma on the cardstock paper as shown in the picture.

7. Make sets of numbered craft sticks, 0 to 9, for each student or group. Label numbers at the top of craft sticks.

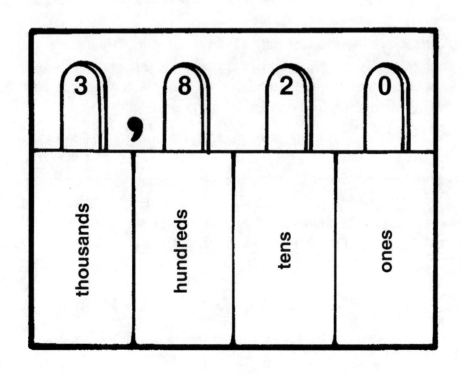

Tips for Math

Place Value Pockets *(cont.)*

Here is another idea for working with place value. Follow the directions below.

1. Get four pocket holders.

2. Cut the four pocket holders to make them slighter smaller on the front only.

3. Label the pocket holders as follows: thousands, hundreds, tens, and ones.

4. Staple them to the poster board, leaving room to mark the commas for separation of place value.

5. Using colorful, unlined index cards, make four sets of 0 to 9. Place a set of 0–9 in each pocket holder as shown below.

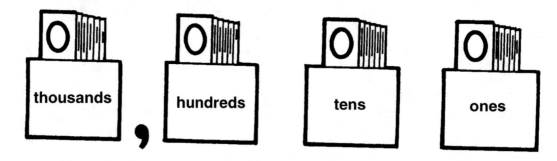

During instruction, the teacher will call out a number. The student must pick the correct number card for each of the place value pockets. Then the teacher will ask other students, "Did this student place the cards correctly?" If not, "Who wants to try to help him (or her) correct it?"

As skills are gained, add more pockets and number sets to the ten thousands, hundred thousands, and millions. Build skill as the different positions are worked on within the classroom. Students also can be tested in the same way but using pencil and paper. The teacher will call out 10 different numbers. The student will write the numbers called, correctly spacing and putting in the comma where appropriate.

Tips for Math

Place Value Bee

Make learning place value into a game called "Place Value Bee." Follow the rules of a spelling bee. Divide the class into groups, calling on each team member with a different number. If missed, the team member sits down and the opposite team member attempts to write the problem correctly.

Block Dice Place Value

Make learning place value into a game using dice. You will need the following materials: four wooden cubes, permanent markers, and protective spray.

Follow the directions below to complete this activity:

1. Make round dots on each cube as you would find on a regular die.

2. Choose two students to each roll two dice.

3. Place the four dice side by side.

4. Call on a student to read the number using all four blocks. (*Note:* There will be multiple ways to write the number. Once the dice are rolled, the numbers can be switched around to change the place value.)

5. Have another student swap the numbers to make a different number place value and continue teaching strategy for reinforcement.

"two thousand five hundred forty-one"

Tips for Math

Transparency Place Value

Often, teachers may find students having difficulty in clearly understanding larger place values. To reinforce the concept of place value, utilize both the auditory and visual modalities of learning.

Students enjoy lessons that include game formats. To alter the mode of instruction, try using the overhead projector to encourage class participation in learning to read and write large numbers.

Follow the directions below.

1. Make a simple visual (as shown below) on a transparency.
2. Call out a given number depending on students' levels (hundreds, thousands, etc.).
3. Have students write the number on a sheet of paper.
4. As you call out numbers, walk around to check for errors.
5. Call on a volunteer to write the number on the transparency.
6. Let the class decide if the number is correctly written.
7. If so, ask the student to read the number written.

$$\underline{\quad 7 \quad} , \underline{\quad 6 \quad} \quad \underline{\quad 2 \quad} \quad \underline{\quad 8 \quad}$$

thousands   **hundreds**   **tens**   **ones**

Door to Rounding Numbers

Use a visual to help students understand rounding. When beginning the teaching of rounding, students will only round to the nearest tens position. Write the number on the board. Draw a line between the ones and the tens and make a door out of the tens position. Underline the ones number. (See example below.) Ask, "Is the underlined number five or more or less than five?" If the number is less than five, change the number to the right of the line to 0. Your answer would be 40.

Example 1 ———— It's less; so I drop the number and make it 0.

4|3 = ___ 4 3 = 40

If the number is five or more, add one to the door.

Example 2 ———— It's more; so I add one to the door.

4|7 = ___ 4 7 = 50

In the subsequent demonstrations and questioning of students, omit the door and just use the line. Follow the same procedure for hundreds and thousands. All numbers to the right of the door become zeros. After initial introduction, phase out the "door" and only use a line. All lines go to the right of the numeral spot that you are to round. For example, if the student is rounding to the nearest thousands, the line would go to the right of the thousand's spot.

Twos, Fives, and Tens Game

For a fun activity to reinforce counting by 2s, 5s, and 10s, use a beach ball, a sponge-type ball, or a bean bag for throwing. Have students get into a circle. The first student begins by calling out a number, for example, "2." Then this student throws the ball or bag to another student and that student must count by 2s to the next number, 4. That student then throws the ball to another student and the sequence continues. The game should be played like the old game of "Hot Potato." No one wants to be left holding the ball when the teacher calls out "Popcorn" or some other word of choice.

Tips for Math

Dot-to-Dot

You can make learning to count by 2s, 5s, and 10s easy and fun. Purchase a simple dot-to-dot book. Using a sheet of paper, trace the dots, leaving off the dot numbers or dot letters used in the book. Then, put whatever number sequence you wish. You might want to make the entire sheet counting by 5s. You can also adapt this idea for sequencing the alphabet. It is a versatile sheet. Be sure you store a duplicate for future use.

Math Baseball

Here is a fun game for drilling on multiplication and division facts. Move back the desks so as to clear a space in the room. Establish first base, second base, third base, and home base. The teacher will act as the pitcher and the students will be the batters. Choose one student to be the scorekeeper and divide the class into teams.

The pitcher will call out a multiplication or division fact. The student has to the count of three to call out the answer. If the student gets the problem correct, the student moves to first base. If the student get the problem wrong, that team gets an out. The scorekeeper will keep the score on the board (score one for each run). The winning team will be the team with the greatest number of runs at the end of the game.

Math Magic

This one is for those younger students who know their multiplication and division facts.

1. Think of a number between 1 and 10.
2. Add 9.
3. Multiply your number by 2.
4. Subtract 4.
5. Divide by 2.
6. Subtract the number you selected from the number you now have.
7. Your answer is 7.

How did the teacher come up with the answer? It works the same way with any number! It is just math magic!

Roll and Multiply

Watch how fast students will learn to multiply with this game. You will need the following materials: poster board, permanent marker, and a die. Divide the poster board into evenly spaced squares. Randomly space numbers 0 to 9 across the board. Laminate for durability.

Now play the game! A student will drop or roll the die onto the poster board. Whatever number is rolled on the die will be multiplied by the number where the dice landed on the board.

Multiplication Roll

To play this game, you will need the following materials: six cardboard toilet paper rolls, one box (about 9" x 12" x 2"), scissors, stapler, glue, and a permanent marker. Follow the directions below to create the game.

1. Cut one 9" x 12" panel from the box.

2. Fit the six toilet paper tubes across the bottom end of the box. If tubes fit evenly, staple tubes together so that they will be anchored.

3. Number each tube.

4. Elevate box on one end by placing a book or other object under it so box is slightly tilted.

Now you are ready to play the game. Each student player will have one roll. Students will roll a small ball into a tube. The ball will go in one tube and come out another. Student will have to multiply the number the ball went in with the number where the ball came out. Keep score. You might wish to divide students into teams, using a game similar to a spelling bee. If an answer is not correct, that student will drop out. Adjust as needed.

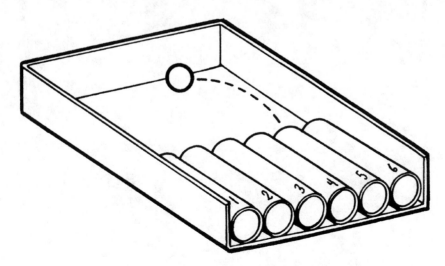

Tips for Math

Multiplication System Idea

This is not a new math trick, just a helpful one. When teaching students to learn the 12s tables, use this system:

12 x 2 = 22 + 2 = 24   12 x 5 = 55 + 5 = 60   12 x 8 = 88 + 8 = 96

12 x 3 = 33 + 3 = 36   12 x 6 = 66 + 6 = 72   12 x 9 = 99 + 9 = 108

12 x 4 = 44 + 4 = 48   12 x 7 = 77 + 7 = 84

Hands Multiplication

This is an old, but sometimes forgotten, math trick to learn the nines multiplication tables. Hold hands in front of you, palms facing outward. The teacher calls out a multiplication problem using nine: 3 x 9. The student begins with the left hand, left side of hand. Count fingers off to the number to be multiplied by 9—"1, 2, 3." Fold down the third finger from the left (the middle finger) as shown below. Look at the hands. You have the answer 3 x 9 is 27; just count your fingers on the left and then the remaining fingers as shown.

Palms Outward

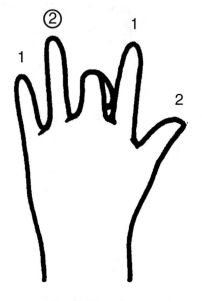

Left Hand

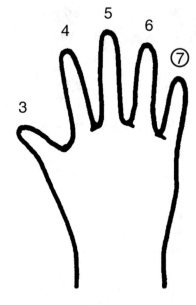

Right Hand

How Much Does It Weigh?

Use a plastic coat hanger, some string, and two plastic plates of equal size and you can have an instrument to show which item weighs more than another item. This is a good hands-on experience for children. Just follow the picture shown to the right and you will be able to use this idea in no time!

Division Chart

Do you ever have trouble teaching the steps of division without the students getting confused? Try this idea. On a large chart, write the four steps in the division process: divide (÷), multiply (x), subtract (−), and bring down (↓). Keep the cue chart on the wall for use by students. Along with this cue chart, the teacher can repeat over and over the process when working with the students to "cement" the learning steps. Remove when the chart is no longer needed. (*Note:* When making reinforcement worksheets, be sure to include the text of the chart on each paper.)

String Measurement

Use string to measure specific items around the classroom. Have students graph according to lengths. For younger students, list certain things for them to measure with string. Have them discuss which is longer or shorter or the same size.

Teaching Estimation

Want to have all students participating in an estimation game? Get the following materials: jars, contact paper, filler (jellybeans, nuts, candy, etc.), and a permanent marker.

Tips for Math

Teaching Estimation *(cont.)*

Take the filler, such as jelly beans, and place them in a pint jar. Cover the lid with contact paper. On the lid write, "Guess Me." Have students estimate how many pieces of the filler are in the jar. The winner gets to carry the jar home at the end of the set period. Be sure that you keep a list of guesses. Allow students only one guess.

You can make seasonal jars. For example, at Halloween, fill the jar with candy corn. At Thanksgiving, use nuts. At Christmas, use peppermints. At Valentine's Day, use candy hearts. You do not always have to have an edible treat in the jar. Use rocks, pencils, dried beans, balls, or marbles. There are a variety of things you can use to fill the jar. For ensuring student interest, have a reward for the winner. For example, if the treat is not edible, it may be that the reward is one or two special passes to "get out of homework," or it may be that the reward is to be line leader for two weeks. The prize will depend on the level of your students.

(*Note:* Be sure to check for food allergies. Be sure that the students only have one chance each period. Keep a list in the back of your lesson plans where students sign and date when each takes a guess.)

Question/Answer Graphing

To have fun in beginning graphing, have students form, groups. Each group will ask specific questions of other students and graph the answers. To make this activity run smoothly, have the students only ask about four to five questions for graphing. Have each group write their questions and get approval from the teacher. Students should understand that the approval is only used for making sure that there are different questions in each group. To show results, make a classroom poster graph, showing questions and answers.

Weather Graphing

Combine science and math by having students graph the weather each day. In order to successfully do this activity, have a classroom outdoor thermometer and an indoor classroom thermometer displayed. Students can keep individual graphs for a specific time period in their notebooks for checking at a later date.

Calendar Graphing

A great way to work with graphing is to obtain a calendar for each student in your class. Have students investigate the calendar by doing the following activities: interviewing classmates for birthdays, locating and highlighting holidays of each month, counting the number of days in each month, and discussing what happened when there is a leap year. After gathering information and studying the calendar, graph the following: number of birthdays in each month, number of holidays in each month, or number of days in each month.

Graphing Shapes

Set up a chart with columns labeled circle, square, rectangle, cylinder, etc. Have students record and graph different geometric solids and shapes around the school. Look at the examples below for ideas.

Square	Rectangle	Cylinder
ceiling tile	door	trash can
window	paper	chalk
bulletin board	book	candle

Play Ball

This is a fun way to learn math tables or work math problems. The cost is minimal to make, but it will be fun for the students. You will need the following materials: cardboard or tagboard for game, markers for game design, game pieces, and a scoreboard. Then follow the directions below.

1. Make a game board showing baseball bases and a pitcher's mound.

2. Write problems to be solved on cardboard squares.

3. Have a scoreboard. This can be a small whiteboard or chalkboard. Divide the board into two teams for scoring.

4. Divide groups into two teams. Rotating, each student will draw a math problem. If the student gets the answer, the students will move to first base. Each problem to be drawn will have a value. The easier problem will be a single run. Problems should vary in runs according to degree of difficulty.

Tips for Math

Odd and Even Days

Try this creative way to teach odd and even numbers. When students are lining up to go to the lunchroom or to the library, use the following system: on days that are odd numbers (Example: March 21), the girls get to go first; on days that are even (Example: March 22), the boys lead the pack. Students will catch on quickly!

Throw It!

Here is a fun game to do with a plastic beach ball. With a permanent marker, write numbers spaced out over the ball. The ball will be thrown to the first student. When the student catches the ball, he or she will add the numbers where his or her hands touched the ball. Play the same game with learning subtraction facts or odd and even numbers.

Pass It On

Divide students into teams of four or five. Give each group one sheet of lined paper. Then have a race. Instructions are given to the groups: "The first person will begin by placing a 2 on the paper. Pass the paper to the person next to you. This person will write the next number counting by twos. The first group that reaches 100 calls out 'Got it!' Let us see which team can count the fastest by twos. Make sure what you write is correct. It will be checked before I give your team the winning prize!"

You can also use this game with counting by 5s or 10s or use this idea to create a new game.

Dominoes

A domino game in your game center is a math plus. Not only are students learning how to play a real game, they must add to make a play! This is also a good game for the teacher to join in on and allow students to catch the teacher making an error.

Fraction Cue Card

A simple way to help students to remember where a numerator and denominator are placed is to make a clue card as follows:

Numerator = North
_____

Denominator = Down South

Once the group has basically caught on to the placement, remove the visual cue card. Otherwise, some students will use it as a crutch.

Pizza Box Fractions

Ask a local pizzeria to donate a number of pizza boxes along with the round cardboard sheets on which pizzas are baked. Using white poster board, draw several circle pizzas that will fit the round cardboard sheets. Add your own drawings of the pizza ingredients. Then, glue the poster board drawings on the round cardboard sheets.

Now, cut each pizza into fractional parts. Cut a pizza into thirds, another into fourths, another into fifths, and so forth. You can use these pizzas for great instructional lessons. For example, to teach that 1/2 is larger than 1/4, show a slice of the 1/2 pizza and compare it to the pizza cut into fourths. Then, ask the students which they would rather have, the 1/2 pizza slice or the 1/4 pizza slice.

Additionally, you can hand a box to a student and ask the student into how many fractional parts the pizza is cut. Have students "eat" part of the pizza. Discuss how much was eaten and how much was left. This is a great visual. Fractions become a functioning part of learning this way.

Plate Fractions

Use different-colored dinner plates. Cut each plate into different sets of fractional parts: halves, thirds, fourths, fifths, sixths, etc. Students can practice identifying and counting by fractional parts with ease. Store them plastic zipper bags.

Tips for Math

Dig Those Fractions

This is a fun way for students to learn fractions. Most of the following materials can easily be found in school or at home: Styrofoam egg carton, knife for cutting, tongue depressors or craft sticks, and a permanent marker. Follow the directions below.

1. Cut off the top half of an egg carton and discard.

2. Turn the egg carton upside down.

3. Cut a small slit in the bottom of each egg cup.

4. On the cup sides, write a fractional amount, such as 3/4, 1/2, etc.

5. Next, obtain craft sticks. On each, draw circles of different fractional amounts.

6. Have the students match the sticks to the fractional amounts on each egg cup.

Restaurant Menus

Using restaurant menus for real-world math can be a nice change for students. Many restaurants have old menus or take-out menus that you can obtain at no charge. Any paper menu should be laminated for durability.

Have students choose items to eat, add menu items, add tax, total and even add a tip for the server. Give each student a certain amount of money to pay for his or her dinner at the restaurant.

Break students in groups of four or five and have each make up an order, put the orders together, add, etc.

Bargain Advertisements

Form whole lessons on multiplication or division skills from all those newspaper grocery advertisements. For example, have a student buy three cans of beans at 59¢ each. Make up a grocery list for the students to complete. The students can figure total prices on what they buy.

Tips for Math

Ad Division

Most multiple magazine offerings come with stamps to attach to the order blank. Save these. You can take the offerings, duplicate, glue to sturdy lightweight cardboard, and make a product for teaching math. Students can do the following activities:

✓ find the cost of each issue of a given magazine

✓ compare final costs for a year's subscription

✓ compare the cost of one magazine against a competing magazine

Price Power

Bring in four items from home such as a box of corn flakes, a can of corn, package of marshmallows, and a bunch of bananas. Write the prices for each item. Have students find the total costs of all the items and add the taxes. (*Note:* Have a tax table made up for the student to use.) Introduce students to the measurements on the items such as lb. and oz.

Create Your Own Ad

Create your own advertisements by cutting and pasting newspaper ads. Then duplicate one sheet per student. Laminate them for durability. Create a list of groceries for students' shopping. Not only is it a good way to teach math skills, it also helps students to see the costs involved when parents have to do the buying!

Timelines

Students often do not understand the meaning of time when it comes to relating the past or future. They seem to live from one day to the next. One way to show time passage is to make a timeline of the school day's activities, beginning with the breakfast program to the ending bell. Have students contribute activities, determining what comes first, second, and so forth. The teacher should do this as a class activity to illustrate the passage of time. Together, the class could make a timeline of the months or special holidays with minimal assistance from the teacher.

Tips for Math

Color-Coded Shapes

Using construction paper, cut out shapes using different colors for each shape: red for a rectangle, blue for a circle, and green for a square. Laminate. After presenting a lesson on shapes and their names, have students form small groups. Have students hunt for items in the shape of a rectangle, a circle, and a square.

Another idea would be to allow the students to place shapes on objects found in and around the school. For example, the red rectangle could be placed on the door, a blue circle on a round table, or a green square on a square bulletin board. The possibilities are limitless. The teacher can help by placing objects around the room. Be sure to inform the principal and other teachers of the project. If the principal has no objection to the activity, be sure to tell the custodians or you could possibly lose your shapes and your activity!

Oil Cloth Shapes

Oil cloth is a life saver! It is durable and will last through many little hands. It is a fun way for younger students to work on learning shapes. Properly made, these shapes will last for many class years. Follow the directions below to make oil cloth shapes.

1. Cut out a number of shapes (squares, rectangles, circles) from the oil cloth.
2. Color code the shapes: red for rectangle, blue for circle, and green for square.
3. Make enough shapes to allow each child to have a set to use.
4. Store sets in plastic zipper bags.

Try calling out the following instructions to the students.

✓ Hold the green square on your nose.

✓ Put the blue circle in your left hand.

✓ Put the red rectangle on your head.

Shape Twister

What about taking larger shapes and placing them on the floor to use for a game similar to Twister™? (*Note:* Learning activities in game format are great, but just remember to keep the noise level down.)

Shape Bead Necklace

Here is a great way to teach shapes and colors to primary students. Gather the following materials: egg cartons, dental floss, dull craft needles, and quick-drying, clear nail polish.

Follow the directions below to assemble the shape bead necklaces:

1. Cut triangles, circles, and squares from egg cartons.

2. Cut a 15-inch thread of dental floss for each student.

3. Thread a single strand of dental floss through a dull craft needle.

4. Secure the end of the thread by tying a knot; then coat the knotted end with quick-drying clear nail polish.

5. Have students string the shapes together following either their own design or a design set by the teacher.

Shape Search

Give students a sheet with "circle," "square," and "rectangle" written across the top. Challenge them to find objects that are found in these shapes. Allow them to question anyone from parents to students outside of their class for answers. Explain that they need to understand what the objects are so they can explain them to other class members if asked to do so. Give this assignment for homework or for a team challenge.

Tips
for
Science

Plants and Growth

To introduce plant growth, use egg carton cups for planting. Other plant holders could be any of the following: large plastic soda bottles cut to size, yogurt cups, or plastic drinking glasses. Seeds that can be used effectively are dry beans, commercial bird seed, alfalfa seeds, acorns, avocado pits, apple seeds, or orange seeds.

To use bean seeds, you will need to rinse beans in cold water. Soak overnight prior to planting. Fill the cup space with potting soil, and then plant seeds.

Most acorns will sprout eventually, but may take longer to show growth. When gathering the acorns, get only those which appear to be in good condition. Remember this tip for using these seeds: keep them in a freezer for about one month prior to use. This helps their growth process. When removed, students should wrap the acorns in damp cotton. Place them in a plastic bag prior to planting in soil. Two sprouts will appear. Plant so that one of the two sprouts will be above the soil and the other under the soil.

With an avocado pit, you will need to insert toothpicks on four sides. The pit is large and can be balanced on a jar's top rim. The pit needs to be partially submerged in water. Check the water level daily as the water is lost through evaporation and absorbed by the plant.

For apple seeds, wrap the seeds in a damp paper towel and place in a plastic zipper bag. Refrigerate for about four to six weeks to allow for germination.

For orange seeds, just plant in potting soil. Water the seeds and cover the container with a plastic bag to create a greenhouse effect. Oranges are grown in warm environments.

Alfalfa and radish seeds should be soaked overnight and then placed between damp paper towels. These seeds need to be kept moist. Put them in a plastic container or zipper bag, but be sure that these seeds have a source of air for growth. Place in a sunny spot.

Tips for Science

Plants and Growth *(cont.)*

To view the seed growth, you will need two panes of glass, paper towels, four large paper clips, and a pan with water.

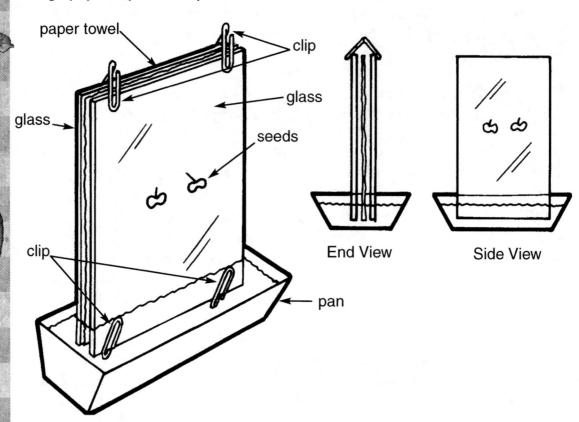

The paper clips will be bent to hold the paper towel and panes of glass together at both the tops and bottom of this experiment. Students can watch the seed growth from between the panes of glass. The paper towel absorbs the water from the bottom of the pan. (*Note:* If you can turn the panes of glass and place them sideways, changing the seeds position, the root of the seeds will change direction as well. In this experiment, beans seem to work the best.)

Be sure to label each seed container if you are using several different types of seeds for variety. Placing wooden craft sticks or tongue depressors in the soil make labeling easy for identification.

Lessons on plant growth can include the following: measuring growth of plants, graphing growth, lessons on what plants need in order to live.

Spring Egg Planters

Use this idea during the year for a fun art project. Save jumbo eggshells and several egg cartons. Crack the jumbo eggshells at the top in order to save as much of the eggshell as possible. Rinse thoroughly and place in an egg carton to save.

After accumulating enough shells, have students draw silly faces on the eggs. Then place potting soil in the eggs. Lightly press rye grass seeds into the soil, and water it. Place in a sunny window area. Soon each silly face will have hair growing and the students laughing. (*Note:* If you do not want to use eggshells, use Styrofoam cups with silly faces. The results will be the same.)

Terrariums

You can easily make a terrarium with a two-liter soda bottle. You will need potting soil and flower seeds to make this project work. Then follow the directions below.

1. Remove the labels and rinse the bottle well. Save the cap to the bottle, as you will secure it to the top of your terrarium.

2. Cut the soda bottle, leaving about 1/3 for the bottom. Some soda bottles have the thick black plastic bottoms. These work best for this project.

3. Cut the top portion in half.

4. Line the bottom with aluminum foil.

5. Fill the bottom 3/4 full of potting soil.

6. Plant seeds or small plants.

7. Water lightly.

8. Add any small objects for decorations if you wish. Small stones or seashells look good in these terrariums.

9. Fit the top portion of the bottle around the bottom. You will find that there will be no need to water these plants!

Tips for Science

Osmosis in Plants

This is a fun experiment to do with younger students. You will need a celery stalk, food coloring, water, and a container. Place the stalk into water; add red food coloring. In about 24 hours, the students will observe that the celery leaves have turned red. Carry the lesson a bit further by using flowers. You can use white daisies, white carnations, or Queen Anne's Lace. Students can observe the flowers as they carry up the colored water. Soon the flowers will take on the color of the food coloring used. Explain to students that all plants need water. Name the simple parts of the plant: the stem, the flower, and leaves. Students learn that the stem carries the water, the flower makes the seeds, and the leaves make the plant's food. Explain that plants will absorb water and minerals through osmosis.

Weather Vane

Students can work on this project together to make a weather vane. The materials needed are as follows: heavy duty aluminum foil, a drinking straw, a piece of cardboard cut from a packing box, and a long nail without much of a head.

Follow the directions below to make the weather vane.

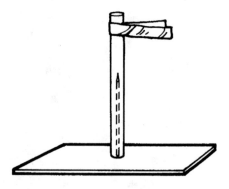

1. Cut a straw into a 4-inch length.

2. Cut a 10-inch by 1-inch length of aluminum foil.

3. Bend the foil around the upper part of the straw, pressing it together tightly.

4. Tape pieces together where they meet and tape the foil to the straw as shown.

5. Secure the nail through the cardboard.

6. Place the straw over the nail.

7. Slightly spread apart the aluminum foil ends.

The weather vane is ready to be tested. When the wind blows, the students will be able to identify the wind's direction.

Teaching Thermometer

You can make a thermometer for teaching purposes. Cut a large piece of poster board, 10' wide and 20' long. Draw a thermometer. Write temperatures by 10s. Draw a line marking increments by 5s.

Make a slit at the top of the thermometer and at the bottom. The slits need to be wide enough to hold and move the ribbon you will attach. Use both red and white grossgrain ribbon for indicating the temperature. You will use about equal amounts of ribbon. Sew ribbons together so that the ribbon can be used to adjust the temperature.

The teacher can call out a temperature while the student moves the ribbon to indicate the temperature. Practice reading the thermometer first in temperatures based on 10s. As students learn to read this thermometer, move on to temperatures by 5s. Talk about the different seasons, kinds of weather, what people wear in warm or cold weather.

Tornado in a Bottle

How about a tornado in a bottle? This experiment needs to be done by the teacher with students watching. You will need a clear two-liter soda bottle, a measuring spoon, several small balls of aluminum foil, some clear liquid soap, and blue food coloring. Then follow the directions below.

1. Drop one teaspoon of liquid soap in the soda bottle.

2. Using the aluminum foil, make four small balls, rolled tightly, and place in the soda bottle.

3. Fill the bottle completely with water.

4. Add several drops of blue food coloring.

5. Rotate the container until the ingredients are swirling.

6. Watch what happens.

The force of the aluminum balls should keep the water swirling. This shows how the movement of our air forms a tornado. Be sure, in your lesson, that you include a discussion of the dangers of a tornado and the safety rules.

Tips for Science

Condensation and Evaporation

Make your own rain inside to teach students about condensation and evaporation.

1. With a permanent black marker, draw a small, simple picture of a lake, surrounded by clouds and trees.

2. Cut the picture to fit inside a small plastic zipper bag.

3. Put the drawing inside the bag.

4. Lay the bag flat and trace over the picture with a permanent marker onto the bag itself.

5. Remove the picture.

6. Add water to the lake level.

7. Seal the bag and tape to a window that receives the sun. The sun will heat the water and air inside the bag. The water will eventually evaporate into the air. Shortly thereafter, the air cannot hold any more water and a demonstration of rain occurs.

Volcano Demonstration

Making a volcano is great for classroom demonstrations. You will need modeling clay to make the volcano shape, scooping out a hole in the top of the volcano. Next, put into the volcano the following: 1 tablespoon of baking soda, several drops of red food coloring, and several drops of a liquid dishwashing soap. Then pour in 1/4 cup of vinegar and watch the action! (*Note*: For easy cleanup, lay down newspaper before beginning demonstration.)

Snowflake Impression

If you have a microscope in your room, this experiment is fascinating. Take a microscope slide and spray it with clear acrylic spray paint. Allow to dry. Lightly spray the slide again until moist. On the slide, catch a snowflake that is falling and place the slide in a cold place, such as a refrigerator. Several hours later, you will find that the spray has dried, the water in the snowflake has disappeared, and you will have the impression of a snowflake. Use your microscope to study it.

Fossil Creations

Want to have students make their own fossils? Have students gather small objects that will make good impressions in the plaster. Suggested objects include leaves, shells, acorns, or twigs. Mix plaster of Paris according to directions. Pour the mixture into a space in an egg carton. Put a light coating of petroleum jelly on the object and press it into the plaster.

A well-known glue company recommends completing this idea in another way. For this experiment, you will need washable school glue or gel, a milk cap, a very small insect that is no longer alive, and aluminum foil. Line the milk cap with foil. Place the insect in the cap. Fill the milk cap with glue, making sure that the insect is covered well.

Next, set the experiment aside and allow to dry for several days. If glue seems to disappear, add more glue and dry completely. This experiment will produce a fake fossil that will give the appearance of an insect trapped in tree sap, like amber, from long ago.

Rock Hardness

After studying the three types of rock, have students decide how hard a rock is. With softer rocks, you will find it easy to scratch the surface with a fingernail. An example of this type of rock would be talc. It will easily crumble. Gypsum and soapstone can be scratched by a fingernail, as well. It just will not crumble as easily. Harder rocks can be scratched with a table knife, pocket knife, a steel file, or concrete nail.

Mineral Content

You can tell if certain minerals are present in rocks. If you want to see if a rock contains calcium, drop a few drops of vinegar onto the rock. If the vinegar bubbles up, you will know that the rock contains calcium.

Tips
for
Social
Studies

Tips for Social Studies

Directions

Students needs to know directions. Make signs for north, south, east, and west and suspend them from your ceiling. Be sure that each sign is pointing in the correct direction. In your lessons, you might want to integrate directions such as "My desk is north of Jimmy's desk. Whose desk is north of Mary's desk?"

Atlantic or Pacific?

Students can remember on which side of the United States the Atlantic Ocean or Pacific Ocean is located by using this trick. The Atlantic Ocean is on the east. To help them remember tell students that the letter A (beginning letter of Atlantic) is nearest the letter E (standing for East). So Atlantic Ocean is on the east. The letter P (beginning letter of Pacific) is nearest W (standing for West). So the Pacific Ocean is nearest West.

School Map

Make a large school map denoting special areas to help orientate the students. You will want to list areas such as the principal's office, the library, the lunchroom, the playground, the water fountains, the bathrooms, and other specific areas. Mark the map with north, south, east, and west. This will help lower elementary students to learn about their environment. Talk about the areas and responsibilities that might accompany each area. Make a small map, without areas marked, for the students to identify where areas are found.

Tips for Social Studies

It's That Big?

Here's an idea for social studies. Many students have no concept of size when it comes to talking about a community, a town, a city, a state, or a nation. In helping students realize size in social studies, use a visual cue as follows:

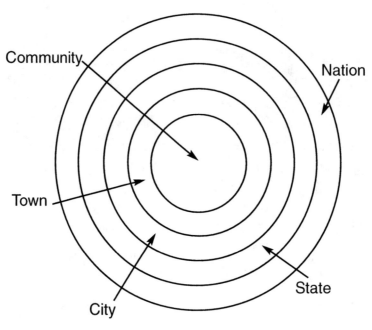

Make each circle a different color. Wrap a lesson around just understanding the size of "where we are."

Simon Says

In helping students remember directions, do not forget the "Simon Says" game. Have students standing unless directed to do otherwise. For learning directions, say, "Simon says for you to point south." "Simon says for you to face east." "Simon says all boys face the south." It is an old idea, but a worthy one.

Tips
for
Art

Tips for Art

Leaf Picture Art

Go on a field trip to collect fall leaves that are just beginning to change color. Place leaves in a plastic zipper bag to keep them moist. When you and the students return, soak the leaves in warm water. Blot dry and place leaves between newspapers to dry. Place heavy books on top of the newspaper to press the leaves. Leave them for one week.

After one week, students can arrange leaves on construction paper and attach with a water-soluble type of glue. Some students may want to make a special placemat by arranging leaves on wax paper. They can cover it with a second sheet of wax paper and the teacher can iron the placemat to seal the two sheets together. Use a pair of zigzag scissors to trim.

An old idea is to spray paint splatter leaf pictures using a screen and a toothbrush. Some teachers feel that using a spray bottle is much easier. (*Caution*: Before you do this, be sure you have enough newspaper to avoid a mess!) Students should wear old shirts or aprons to protect their clothing as this can be quite messy!

Leaf Rubbings

Make several templates of leaves using different leaf shapes and following the directions below.

1. Outline the leaf's shape and its vein with a black marker.

2. Carefully cover the lines of each leaf with a thin stream of glue.

3. Students can use these patterns to make "rubbings" of leaves. You can discuss the veins of the leaves and how water passes through these veins or discuss how the leaf makes food for the plant.

If the lesson is near Thanksgiving, have students write something for which they are thankful on their leaves. You can also have students write a rule for good manners on the leaf.

Tips for Art

Piggy Bank

When working on your money unit, develop an art project to reinforce the concept of money. You can make piggy banks using the following materials: empty bleach bottle, pink felt, empty thread spools, black felt, and pipe cleaners.

Follow the directions below to make the piggy bank.

1. Use the neck of the bleach bottle as the head and nose of the pig.
2. Place thread spools for the four legs.
3. Make ears from pink felt and eyes from black felt.
4. Add a curly tail made with a pipe cleaner.
5. When finished, cut a wide slit in the top for a money drop.

Tooth Boxes

What do you do with a student who loses a tooth at school? You will want to put it in a safe place for the student to take home. Save tiny mint boxes and decorate them. Most mint boxes you find are plastic. How are you going to decorate it? Here is a tip for painting on plastic. If you need to make paint stick to plastic, simply add some white glue to your paint and mix. If by accident, you add too much glue and the paint becomes too thick, just add water as needed. Keep these "tooth" savers for when needed.

Stained Glass Windows

Have students draw designs on white paper. Color the designs. Next, brush cooking oil on the backs of the designs. Wipe off excess oil. Hang on monofilament line across the windows.

Window Clings

You can make window clings by using thin transparency sheets, school glue, food coloring, and templates. Mix food coloring with glue. Students can then paint with the glue by putting a design under the thin sheet and then copying the design. When this is completed, place the design in a safe spot to dry overnight. Drying should be a minimum of twelve hours. After completely dried, you can peel off the design and it will adhere on a window. Your window clings are complete!

Tips for Art

Line Pictures

For kindergarten or first grade students who need to improve fine motor coordination skills, make your own line pictures to follow. Just take a beginning coloring book, a sheet of tracing paper and a sheet of carbon paper. Use a tracing wheel to trace over the picture. Duplicate and you are ready to go.

Learning About Color

Save those round potato chip cans. You will find them to be very useful. For a display to help students learn color words, wrap each can in a color: blue, red, yellow, green, orange, white, black, purple, etc. Using a black marker, give the covered cans the appearance of crayons, complete with markings. For the pointed part of the crayon, just use construction paper or poster board folded to make a point. Not only will you be providing a good method for teaching color words, you will have a 3-D effect as well!

Colors, Colors, Colors

Make fall come into focus with this colorful idea. For a class project you will need coffee filters, small plastic containers, different food colors, paper towels, scissors, and newspaper. Set up the project with coffee filters, tubs, and food coloring. Give each student a coffee filter. Have him or her fold the filter at least twice. He or she will dip the edge and center of the coffee filter into the food coloring located in the plastic containers. You may have to demonstrate these directions. The fibers in the filters will move the flow of color. After dipping the filters, students will press the filters between paper towels to absorb any remaining liquid. Allow filters to dry. The finished project can be used for making borders on bulletin boards, for door decoration, or just for students to take home!

Classroom Globe

Make a classroom globe with a balloon and strips of paper. Blow up a round balloon. Attach strips using papier maché paste of flour and water. When dry, paint with blue tempera. Pop the balloon. Have students cut out continents out of paper. Attach the continents to the sphere with glue and suspend from the ceiling.

Ice Cream Learning Cones

Have each student put three scoops of "paper ice cream" on top of a brown paper cone. On each scoop, have the students write what they are learning. You could add a magnet and have it ready to take home and put on the refrigerator.

Shape Templates

Need templates for an art activity? Try the following ideas:

- ✓ Use coffee-can plastic lids for large circles.
- ✓ Use small plastic dessert plates for medium-sized circles.
- ✓ Use potato chip plastic lids for smaller circles.
- ✓ Use old CDs for circles.
- ✓ Use a shoebox top for drawing large rectangles.
- ✓ For a small rectangle, use a matchbox.
- ✓ For squares, use a ceramic tile or square box lid.

CD Suncatcher

Want an eye appealing sun catcher? Glue two CDs together. The shiny sides pick up all sorts of color reflections. To hang, the teacher will have to use some type of object that can be heated to make a hole through the two discs. Now you are ready to put twine or decorative ribbon through the holes for hanging.

Sewing Cards

Many very young children have not developed good muscle coordination. This fun activity will help improve their coordination. Sewing cards can be made from Styrofoam trays. The design can be as simple as lacing the straight-line shape of trays, or more complicated ones that you have created. You may want to cut off the side portions of the tray, making it completely flat. You can also cut the Styrofoam trays into shapes.

Use yarn for sewing. To make the yarn's ends more manageable, dip the ends in candle wax. Before it cools completely, form pointed ends. Drape the yarn on a coat hanger to dry. Sometimes it is helpful to tape the ends tightly. Some teachers prefer to dip the yarn in white glue or clear fingernail polish and shape the point.

Tips for Art

Bird Feeders

It is not a new idea to make bird feeders for the feathered friends, but here are several types for you to consider for a class project.

1. Take an aluminum pie pan. Punch two holes on the lip of the pie pan, making the holes about two inches apart. Then, hole punch the other side in the same way. Fill with birdseed and tie it on a limb with string looped through the holes.

2. A second way would be to use 1/2 gallon milk cartons. Use a guide to cut out windows on four sides. The teacher can mark the windows on the feeder and let the students finish the cutting. On the bottom portion of the feeder, you will have to cut out a space for inserting sticks for perches. Secure the perches with hot glue. On the folded upper part of the milk carton, punch two holes for twine for hanging. Insert twine and tie the knot. If you lightly sandpaper the feeder, you will find that you can paint the feeder more easily. Now, add birdseed, hang, and watch!

3. Make a pinecone feeder for the birds. Get a very large pinecone. Tie a cord to the cone for hanging it on a limb. Then, make the food for the birds. You will need vegetable shortening, corn meal, and some birdseed. Mix it all together and cover the pinecone. If you want to add more food, birds love things like chopped nuts and sunflower seeds.

Sticker Creations

Did you know that you can make your own stickers? It is easy to do, if you can spare the time. All you need is the following two ingredients: 1/4 cup of white glue and 1 tablespoon of vinegar. Follow the directions below.

1. Mix well 1/4 cup of white glue with 1 tablespoon of vinegar in a plastic tub.

2. Next, cut pictures from cards, magazines, or wallpaper.

3. Brush the back of each picture with the mixture.

4. Let dry with the picture side down.

5. After the pictures dry, you can wipe the back of a sticker with a damp sponge.

6. Now, you can put the sticker wherever you wish!

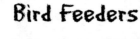

Tips
for
Centers

Tips for Centers

Introduction

Centers are a good method for teaching students to effectively work individually, collectively, and to assume responsibility. All centers are designed to be teaching areas. Remember that they should be set up to meet the curriculum needs of your class and school. Centers can be designed to cover any area of study: listening, silent reading, spelling, math, or possibly as an art center. Developing these centers requires time and organization on the part of the teacher. Centers should be a non-intimidating environment where the student learns to work independently and without direct teacher intervention. Students should be able to find materials on their own. They should be inviting to your students. Feel free to change the centers whenever students' interest seem to be waning. Make centers a fun and good learning experience for your students.

Here are some things you might want to include in a center:

✓ hole punch	✓ puzzles	✓ rulers
✓ scissors	✓ dry erase board	✓ easel
✓ markers	✓ plastic counters	✓ play money
✓ pencils	✓ games	✓ clocks
✓ paste	✓ microscope	✓ brushes
✓ pattern blocks	✓ timers	✓ books
✓ measuring cups	✓ scrap material	✓ blank paper
✓ crayons	✓ calculators	✓ graph paper
✓ measuring tools	✓ letter stencils	✓ magazines
✓ hourglass	✓ thermometer	✓ magnets
✓ colored pencils	✓ tape recorder	✓ dice

Keeping Clean and Neat

Having problems keeping the learning centers clean and uncluttered? A simple way to stop center cluttering is to put a "Closed for a Week" sign on the center. First, none of the students will want the centers to be closed. Second, the students will not be happy with the ones who left the center messy. Third, the students will learn to monitor their own classmates in keeping the centers clean!

To make this work well, be sure that you establish and discuss rules for keeping your centers organized and clean. Place the responsibility on the students, not the teacher.

Storage for Materials

Store manipulatives and other materials in many different storage containers. Any can that has a plastic lid will be good for storage in a learning center. Having storage containers will also allow students to take center materials back to their desks if other students are using the center.

Some good items for storage are as follows:

- ✓ plastic zipper bags
- ✓ coffee cans
- ✓ sturdy ice cream canisters
- ✓ potato chip cans
- ✓ film canisters
- ✓ formula cans
- ✓ garbage bags (Great for storing large posters and bulletin board materials.)
- ✓ clothesline in a corner to hang each bag using clothespins (This provides for moveable learning centers when you are short on space in the classroom.)

Tips for Centers

Pretend Center: Different Lands

Younger students love to pretend, so why not create an area where they can pretend to be different characters in different lands? This center should be used primarily on rainy days or during a room break when activities must stay inside.

For Hawaii, you can make hula skirts out of brown paper grocery bags by following the directions below.

1. First, open the closed end of the bag.

2. Lay flat.

3. Draw lines to cut strips of paper for the grass skirt.

4. Mark off about three inches at the top.

5. Make shoulder straps from a second bag.

6. Play a CD or cassette of Hawaiian music. Your students would love it!

Pretend Center: King (or Queen)

How about making crowns for the king or queen? They can easily be made from empty bleach bottles.

1. Measure a band about 6 inches around the center of the bleach bottle.

2. Cut out the band.

3. Cut out triangles from the band to make the crown.

4. Spray paint with gold paint.

5. Decorate with old jewelry or jewelry stones from a craft store.

You can adjust the band size to fit the students by clipping, cutting, and restapling the crown to fit the head.

Pretend Center: Trains and Castles

Grab those large boxes such as those in which refrigerators and other large appliances are packaged. For a castle, follow the directions below.

1. Cut out the bottom of the box.

2. Stand the box with open parts up.

3. Take the cardboard and curve it around.

4. Staple tower together and attach to the corners.

5. Spray paint for effect and add small windows, an entrance gate with markers, etc.

For a train, you will need one large box and one or more smaller boxes. The larger box becomes the engine and "engineer's spot."

1. Cut out the engineer's windows.

2. Make a smoke stack out of cardboard.

3. Staple together and put on engine.

4. Cut out wheels and glue on the train. You could use paper or aluminum pie plates to serve as wheels.

5. Then, invite people to come aboard!

Pretend Center: Safari

Save those toilet paper rolls to make binoculars for your safari center. Follow the directions below to make binoculars.

1. Take two toilet paper rolls and cover them with black construction paper and glue. (*Note:* You may want to spray paint the binoculars instead of using the black paper.)

2. Use rubber bands to hold the construction paper on the toilet rolls.

3. Glue some type of small spacer between the two tubes for separating them enough to fit the eyes

4. Then hole punch two holes in the binoculars and use yarn or ribbon for the strap.

Tips for Centers

Pretend Center: Photographer

Make your own camera for the student who wants to play photographer by using the following materials: small cereal box, tape, construction paper, toilet tissue tube, scissors, yarn, and lids to medicine bottles, brads, or buttons. Follow the directions below.

1. Take a small cereal box.

2. Seal all open areas with tape.

3. Cover box with construction paper.

4. Cover a toilet tissue tube with the same construction paper.

5. Cut a hole in the cereal box and insert the tube into it.

6. Add your dials and switches with lids to medicine bottles and buttons. Brads poked through the camera could also serve as dials.

7. Use yarn to hang the camera around the neck.

Pretend Center: Music Band

Have a pretend band playing with the following pretend instruments.

✓ *Drum*—Use large three-pound coffee cans with plastic lids. Spray paint them, if you wish. Punch holes in the sides of the can to thread a string through so the student can wear the drum around the neck. Open both ends of the drum. Add plastic lids on both ends.

✓ *Cymbals*—Get two pot lids and use these for cymbals. The lids should be the same size and have top handles that are easy for the student to hold.

✓ *Kazoo*—You can easily make a kazoo with a comb and a piece of tissue paper. Wax paper also works. Just fold a piece of tissue paper over the comb. Put the kazoo up to the lips and hum away.

✓ *Pipe Organ*—You can even have a pipe organ. Use glasses filled with different levels of water. The different levels will produce different sounds. Students will enjoy exploring the making of sounds with this instrument.

Pretend Center: Music Band *(cont.)*

✓ *Tambourines*—Take two aluminum pie pans. Take your hot glue gun and glue 3/4 of the way around. Add small dried beans inside. Finish gluing the pans together. Take another aluminum pan. Cut out small circles. Punch holes in the center of the circles and attach to the tambourine at the outer edges. You will have to punch holes at the outer edge of the double pie pans to hold the small circles. Attach circles with colorful yarn.

✓ *Guitar*—Make a guitar with a cigar box and several different sized rubber bands. Remove the top from the cigar box. Insert small-headed nails on the outer lengthwise rims of the cigar box. Leave enough room to stretch a rubber band between the two outer rims.

✓ *Castanets*—Make castanets by holding two spoons together so that the rounded part of each spoon faces each other. Place one spoon between the thumb and the knuckle of the first finger. The second spoon will rest between your first and second finger. Hit them together against the leg. When they hit each other, they sound like castanets.

✓ *Maraca*—Use drink or juice containers with plastic lids. Add seeds for a maraca.

Pretend Center: Grocery Store

Accumulate empty cans from home and bring them to school for your grocery unit. Make your shelves from cardboard boxes turned upside down. Cover with contact paper. Label areas with letters of the alphabet. Have students stock the groceries according to letters. (Example: Have a B section where the students will place items such as beans, beets, and bananas; a C section for corn, cereal, cream, and cabbage.)

For empty wall space in your center, use grocery store fliers on the wall. Remind students that in order to buy at a grocery place, you need money. You might want to laminate the paper money for durability. Use old wallets and purses for the shoppers.

Tips for Centers

Pretend Center: Playhouse

For your playhouse center, the table in the center can be decorated with place mats that you make yourself. All you need is some scrap oilcloth and cut away! Primary students can practice setting a table along with their other chores.

Gardening Center

A gardening center can be a great learning experience for all children. Use two-liter drink bottles. The bottom black part makes a good planter. Or empty milk cartons also make good containers.

Get permission from your principal and begin an outdoor flower garden. Students will love seeing the results of their efforts. At the end of the unit, the students can take home their plants.

Poetry Center

You may wish to set up a poetry center. You will want to have a book of rhyming words for students to use. Loose-leaf paper should be included. One fun way to introduce poetry to students is to rhyme their own names. Some names are too difficult to be rhymes, so allow the students to pick another name or to use their middle or last name.

Reading Center

A reading center is like a library center. You should have an inviting place to read. Be sure that your center has a good collection of books. You do not really need to have a bookcase. You can put books in colorful boxes or baskets!

Have a magazine corner. Magazines can be a good source of many activities. If you do not have access to a display rack, make your own. Using a piece of pegboard or tagboard, make pockets to hold magazines. Use a clear plastic front so students can see the covers. Covers will draw interest. Magazines can be used for cutting out pictures, words, advertisements; finding headlines; and many other kinds of activities.

Writing Center

In the writing center you should have many different writing tools, from chalkboards to dry erase boards to paper. In the center, your materials should include paper that has lines, some that is unlined, colored paper, different sizes of index cards, old manila folders, felt boards. Along with these tools, have an idea box of interesting things to write about. Have story starters for students to use.

Some other things to include in the writing center are as follows:

✓ *Mailbox*— The writing center should be fun, so why not have a mailbox? Put the flag up to show mail is in the box. Students can write special letters to special people. Set up a time of the day for delivery.

✓ *Greeting Cards*—Include construction paper and colored pencils so students can design and write greeting cards.

✓ *Reference Books*—No writing center would be complete without dictionaries and a thesaurus. If you are lucky enough to have a set of encyclopedias, you can include them in the writing center.

✓ *Alphabet Stamp Markers*—Students will enjoy stamping their spelling words as they study.

✓ *Box of Laminated Writing Ideas*—Have different kinds of writing for the students to choose from such as the following: newspaper reporting, imagination writing, biographical times, research writing, etc.

The kinds of writing you will keep in your center will depend on the ages of the students. Remember that many things appeal at different ages and levels of the students. For example, a story on going to a zoo would be appropriate for younger elementary students. However, a story on a special football team would be of special interest to the older elementary student.

Tips
for
Decorating

128

Tips for Decorating

Introduction

The key to a well-decorated room is this—educate, do not just decorate. Never put up bulletin boards just because you have to—they can be extremely effective teaching tools.

Bulletin Board Backgrounds

Bulletin boards do make our rooms look colorful and bright. Think about the backgrounds for bulletin board placements. There are so many things you can use in a creative way to enhance any and all bulletin boards. My favorite is to use a colorful fabric. Fabric can be easily stored with little space. Go to your favorite fabric store and find something to use for your background. You may want to choose denim or any other type of solid-colored material. Prints can be used, but be careful as they may get too busy for the eye!

Try sponge painting. You can add color to a faded board. Your print can be either seasonal or non-seasonal.

Some other ideas for backgrounds include the following:

- ✓ book covers
- ✓ travel ad posters
- ✓ maps
- ✓ tablecloths
- ✓ wrapping paper
- ✓ newspaper
- ✓ butcher paper
- ✓ comic pages
- ✓ wallpaper
- ✓ grocery ads
- ✓ fruit mesh bags
- ✓ stretched poly-fill batting sheets
- ✓ shower curtains

Tips for Decorating

Bulletin Board Backgrounds *(cont.)*

These can be easily attained and with little or no expense. Additionally, you might wish to laminate some of these for durability and strength.

You can also use many items to spice up your bulletin boards, but be creative. For instance, try using old sheets draped in a particular shape. Try adding balloons in one corner. Try using wadded-up pieces of cellophane. Add texture of any kind. Up goes your theme and you have not only a different kind of board but a far more interesting one!

Bulletin Board Borders

Adding color and dimension to a border will enhance your bulletin board's eye-catching appeal. Try these ideas that will add both interest and color to your board.

- ✓ paper grass such as those used in Easter baskets
- ✓ tinsel left from holiday season
- ✓ leaves
- ✓ leftover craft raffia
- ✓ old greeting cards laced in crossed positions and connected together
- ✓ laminated strips of fabric
- ✓ cartoons glued to a border line
- ✓ measuring tapes for a math measurement board
- ✓ sentence strip paper with student names
- ✓ foil baking cups
- ✓ large puzzle pieces glued to a strip of construction paper
- ✓ poster board
- ✓ bookmarks glued and angled together
- ✓ different-colored construction paper, placed at odd angles

Bulletin Board Borders *(cont.)*

A very different idea is to use vines for borders. It makes a board most unusual and decorative. For a title, you could say. "I Heard It Through the Grapevine . . . ."

Additionally, you could make a border out of popped popcorn and use the title: "Look Who Popped In!" and place the students' school pictures on the bulletin board.

At Christmas and Hanukah season, use magnolia leaves for a border. They will easily retain shape and color for a 3-D effect. Do the same for fall leaves by spraying leaves with an acrylic clear spray. You can collect leaves and soak them in glycerin for about 24 hours. The glycerin preserves the leaves and makes them pliable.

Another 3-D idea would be to use the following items for borders. (*Note*: Small patches of Velcro on your bulletin boards can be very useful. Use the Velcro to hold up many of your items in use.)

- ✓ empty creamer containers
- ✓ bubble wrap
- ✓ Styrofoam packing peanuts
- ✓ crumpled newspapers
- ✓ lightweight cord

Think Color

Think of color in a bulletin board. We associate red with the border of valentines. Have a theme such as "Think Red." Have student add to the making of the board by naming (or illustrating) all things that we associate with the color red. Do the same for the month of March with green. In the month of October, use fall colors of yellows and browns.

Tips for Decorating

Lettering

You will not always have to use those commercially-made letters for your boards, try making your own out of wallpaper books. Laminate the sheet of paper and cut away. It is easy and at no cost to you. Stores selling wallpaper will often give you the books at no cost.

Make your letters out of fabric. They are durable, will last, and be different. Before cutting, use liquid starch to stiffen the material. Let dry and trace your letters straight onto the material. Students love to cut out bulletin board letters. If you have some "good cutters," pass the task to these students and give yourself some extra time to work with other students. (*Helpful Hint:* Do you have trouble putting up the letters on your bulletin board when you want them in a straight line? Simply use thumbtacks and a string to show the way.)

Using Hot Glue

A hot glue gun is handy to have when you are putting up your posters. Did you know that you can use a hot glue gun to stick posters to stucco or cold brick walls? It will easily peel off when you are through with the display.

If a poster is not laminated, reinforce the corners with book tape so glue will not adhere directly to the poster. Be smart and laminate your posters. Hot glue will not stick or smear like other products do on a laminated poster. Also, it will not leave holes in the wall.

Hanging from Tiles

If you have acoustical tiles in your classroom, you can hang lightweight items with an unbent paper clip, tucking one end under the metal supports holding the tiles in place. Then attach what you want to hang using monofilament fishing line.

Sports Bulletin Board

Do not forget sports! There is football, basketball, baseball, soccer, hockey, and many other sports. Have a sports board. Let students bring in pictures of their favorite baseball player or basketball player to put on the board.

Tips for Decorating

January: Snowflakes

Have students fold paper to make patterns of snowflakes. (*Note:* Be sure to have a broom ready!) Hang these snowflakes from the ceiling on monofilament fishing line.

January: Marshmallow Snowmen

For an art project, make snowmen out of marshmallows attached together with toothpicks. Add buttons with a marker. The nose for the snowman may be made from poster board or construction paper. With a marker, color a miniature marshmallow black for the hat. The rim of the hat may be made from a circle of black construction paper. (*Note:* Warn students not to eat these due to the marker.)

February: Silhouettes

February is the month of presidents. Cut silhouettes of Lincoln and Washington from black construction paper. Then using a bright light, have students make silhouettes of themselves. Develop a thematic unit on futures and pasts, bringing in the lives of past presidents and talking about the futures of your students. You might even want to consider writing on the silhouette cut-paper. It will add to the room décor and students can take pride in their displays.

February: Valentine's Day

You can decorate with hearts and cupids. A fun idea is to take white-ribbed ribbon and red-ribbed ribbon and curl the lengths. Then hang the ribbon curls from your ceiling on monofilament line. Attach valentines and cupids to the ribbons.

March: Kites

March is a good month to have students make kites. Lay out a newspaper pattern to help with cutting out the kites. Have students design their kites and decorate them. Use yarn on the kites for string. Attach kites to the ceiling with monofilament fishing line and small white clothespins.

Tips for Decorating

April: Spring Flowers

With April comes spring and the budding of trees. It is a good time to teach about new life in science. You can decorate your room with this art project.

1. Take your students on a walk.
2. Have them collect wild flowers.
3. Preserve the flowers.
4. Using a tall juice can, cut up small bits of paraffin.
5. Fill a pot with a small amount of water. Place the can with paraffin inside the pot.
6. Put on low heat and allow the paraffin to melt.
7. When the paraffin is melted, let it cool until it is lukewarm.
8. Next, hold the stem of the flower.
9. Coat the flower with paraffin.
10. Turn the flower up and allow the paraffin to set for a few minutes.
11. Immediately dip the flower in cold water to fully harden.
12. When it dries, the flower will look waxy and lovely.

April: Butterflies

You can make beautiful butterflies to hang in your room using coffee filters. This could be a spring activity or an anytime arts and crafts project. You will need pipe cleaners for the butterfly's body and antenna, coffee filters for the wings, and markers for color. Have the students use the markers to add designs for the butterfly wings. Attach the wings to a hanger and spray with water. (If you feel students will be too messy with the bottle sprayer, use an eye dropper to drop water over the filters.) The water will make the colors spread and run together. Whenever the filter is dry, wrap a pipe cleaner around the body, leaving enough of the pipe cleaner to make antennas. You can suspend these butterflies from the ceiling for a colorful addition to your room.

Tips for Decorating

April: Showers

For your April bulletin board, use an umbrella and drops of rain. Use the umbrellas to emphasize a skill in language such as synonyms, antonyms, or homonyms. Have the most common words, such as the word *pretty*, on the umbrella. Have synonyms as the drops of rain (i.e., beautiful, lovely, gorgeous, attractive).

April: Sun Catchers

Here is another good idea for April. Have students make sun catchers out of clear vinyl, colored cellophane, and glue sticks. After cutting them out, stick them to the window. They will look great!

Easter: Hanging Eggs

Obtain plastic eggs that are sold in packs of twelve. Get some inexpensive ribbed ribbon that can be curled. Cut the ribbon to a "hanging length" and snap into the eggs about four to five inches above the end. Take scissors and make ribbon curls on the ends. Suspend the eggs from your classroom ceiling using monofilament line. This makes for an easy and colorful room decoration.

Easter: Coffee Filter Eggs

Want a cute way to make colorful Easter eggs for a bulletin board? Use coffee filters. Give a filter to each student. Then, have each students color the filter with different colored markers. Use a water dropper to pinch out water drops all over the top of the filter. The colors will run into each other. Let dry overnight. The following day, allow students to cut out each filter in the shape of an egg. Use these on your bulletin board or attach to your windows. The "water drop eggs" will add a special glow to the room. Another idea is to use the Easter eggs to make a border for your Easter board or a door.

Tips for Decorating

May: American Flag

May is always a hard month as school is nearing the end and both the teacher and the students are restless. Here is a good project for Memorial Day.

1. Use red, white, and blue construction paper to make an American flag.

2. Cut out strips of each color: 28 strips of blue, 54 strips of red, and 48 strips of white. These will be made into paper chains.

3. To put the flag together you will follow this pattern:

   ✓ Make seven blue chains of 4 paper strips each.

   ✓ Make four red chains, 6 paper strips each.

   ✓ Make three white chains, 6 paper strips each.

   ✓ Make three white chains, 10 paper strips each.

   ✓ Make three red chains, 10 paper strips each.

You will need to use a mount such as the bulletin board to make the flag. When you have the paper chain flag on the bulletin board, add 50 cutout stars for completion. It is a colorful and fun decoration, plus it is a board that the students have made, not you!

September: Ceiling Hangings

September is not a hard month to decorate for there are so many things one can use. The problem with September decorations is "lack of time." You can hang any of these from the ceiling.

   ✓ pencils

   ✓ paper

   ✓ notes

   ✓ rulers

   ✓ numbers

   ✓ letters

Tips for Decorating

October: Spiders

Take several black garbage bags. Fill one bag with newspaper or other lightweight material. Secure this bag to the ceiling in the center of your room. (*Note:* Monofilament wire is a life saver.) Next, take remaining garbage bags and cut them into six strips for the spider's legs. Attach these to the filled body and attach ends of legs across the room.

October: Spider Web Board

The month of October is a good time to make a bulletin board that can represent a spider web. Center the web to one end of the bulletin board. This is a good time to have "spooky" creative writing, such as the following:

✓ One night I saw a ghost. This ghost was a friendly ghost that . . .

✓ Today I saw something that was scary. It was so scary that . . .

✓ There is a house in our town that people say is haunted. It is . . .

✓ One dark night when I was camping, I heard . . .

October: Bats in the Belfry

Every classroom needs bats for October! Begin with two black construction paper circles each about 5" in diameter. One circle will be the body of your bat. Cut the other circle in half with zigzag lines for the wings. Make a small slit in the top and attach monofilament line or string to hang from the ceiling.

October: Pumpkin Patch

Make your own Halloween pumpkin patch. Have each student bring in a pumpkin (small or large size). Have students decorate the faces of their own pumpkins using markers, stickers, or construction paper. Place the pumpkins around your room.

Tips for Decorating

November: Classroom Teepee

Students will love to make this a part of their Indian-Thanksgiving unit! They will enjoy going into a teepee to read or talk quietly.

You can make a classroom teepee that will provide a lasting memory for your students using the following materials: 6 wooden stakes (8 feet in length), plaster of Paris, brown butcher paper or bulletin board paper, tempera paint for decorations, cord or heavy-duty material for binding, and small cans.

Follow the directions below.

1. Using 8-foot stakes, attach them securely at the top. (Height will allow students to be able to enter.)
2. Spread out the legs to form a teepee.
3. Secure the bottoms of the stakes by putting them in small cans filled with wet plaster of Paris.
4. Leave overnight to harden.
5. Cover the teepee sides with brown butcher paper or bulletin board paper.
6. Have students use tempera paint to make Indian designs on their teepee.

November: Giving "Thanks"

A special project can be developed during the Thanksgiving season. Have each student tell for whom and for what they are thankful. Students can write "thanks" on a cutout of their handprint, on a valentine-shaped heart, or on a turkey feather.

December: Suspended Ornaments

Using unbreakable Christmas ornaments, attach monofilament fishing line. Use the line to suspend the Christmas ornaments from your ceiling. It is attractive, colorful, and different!

December: Peppermint Special

Decorate your room with peppermints that students make using these materials: paper plates, stapler, red ribbon, peppermint extract, red tempera paint, plastic wrap, and cotton balls.

Follow the directions below.

1. Mark the center of two plates. Draw light lines, dividing the plates into eight sections.

2. Have each student paint every other section of two plates red.

3. Staple the two plates together, leaving an opening at the top.

4. Soak about five cotton balls (for each student) in the peppermint extract. Wrap each individually in small pieces of plastic wrap.

5. Stuff these between the two plates. Staple the open section of the two plates together.

6. Tear off two pieces of plastic wrap, long enough to cover the two plates and leave wrapping at the end.

7. Cover the two plates and tie at the end with ribbon to give the effect of peppermint candy.

8. Hang in the room or attach to the wall for a colorful effect.

December: Christmas Elves

Cut a triangle from green construction paper. Cut two arm pieces and two leg pieces out of remaining green paper. Cut out boots from black construction paper. Take pink or white construction paper and cut a small circle for the face and two hands. Add eyes with black felt marker and cotton for the beard. Make a small hole to thread yarn through and you have an ornament for your tree. If you wish, decorate with sparkles. It makes for a colorful elf for your decorated tree.

Tips for Decorating

December: Wreaths

You can have students make this simple wreath. You will need plain paper plates for this project, along with green tempera paint and red yarn. Cut out the inside of the plate. The rim of the plate serves as the wreath. Have students paint their wreaths green. After drying, wrap red yarn around the plate rim and tie into a bow at the top. Students can add colorful decorations with drops of fabric paint. Just place drops randomly. If you use red, the red drops will serve as holiday berries.

You may wish to try this project for your wreath. Have each student trace around his or her hand on green construction paper. Have each student cut out his or her hand. Use the hands to make a circular wreath. Add a red bow and you are set to put up your student wreath.

December: Student Gifts

This recipe makes spiced tea. It can be made in the classroom and put into small baby food jars that students can decorate. (Suggestion: If you use this recipe, see if you can get some of the parents to volunteer to send a few recipe items. The recipe may be costly, if you do not.)

Ingredients

- ✓ 2 26-ounce jars of Tang®
- ✓ 1 cup sugar
- ✓ 2 teaspoons of nutmeg
- ✓ 2 teaspoons of cinnamon
- ✓ 2 8 1/2-ounce pkgs. of Red Hots
- ✓ 2 teaspoons of ground cloves
- ✓ 1 6-oz. package of instant lemonade
- ✓ 2 teaspoons of allspice
- ✓ 1 3-ounce bottle of unsweetened instant tea

Directions

Simply mix all ingredients and place in jars. Directions for the recipe's use: Fill a cup with hot water. Mix in two to three tablespoons of mix to taste.

Tips for Decorating

Year-Round Seasonal Tree

Find a small tree branch that you can make into a tree. Spray paint the tree white. Secure the tree branch in a clay pot filled with florist foam or plaster of Paris. Decorate the clay pot with ribbon and/or designs suitable to be carried forth throughout the year. The tree ornaments can be changed each month with different themes and ideas. Some ornament suggestions are as follows:

✓ *September:* school bells, books, pencils, papers, school houses, flags, stars, desks, apples, rulers, globes, footballs

✓ *October:* bats, friendly ghosts, Columbus' ships, pumpkins, fall leaves, scarecrows

✓ *November:* Pilgrims, corn, cornucopia, fruit, turkeys, corn stalks, ears of corn

✓ *December:* Hanukah candles, Christmas wreaths, candy canes, Christmas ornaments, stockings

✓ *January:* snowmen, snowflakes, silhouettes of Martin Luther King

✓ *February:* Lincoln hats, hatchets, cherries, valentines, groundhogs

✓ *March:* Easter eggs, flowers, kites, shamrocks

✓ *April:* Easter eggs, raindrops, umbrellas, flowers, ducks

✓ *May:* sand pails and shovels, sun, fish, camping tents, cars, ice cream cones

Colorful Cones

A cute way to post colors and color words is to make a large ice cream cone with colorful scoops of ice cream. Write the color word on each scoop.

Miscellaneous Tips

Miscellaneous Tips

Symbols in the Directions

So many times students do not read directions on their papers. In developing worksheets emphasize the direction by drawing a circle around the word, *circle*, or draw a line under the word, *underline*. This helps students to focus on what they are to do.

Which Bus?

Younger children are often confused and frightened about which bus they ride to get home. Help ease the situation by assigning bus tickets to each student riding the bus. Confer with the driver first so the driver knows that is being done.

1. Make a bus drawing. This drawing will be taped to the first inside window of the bus.

2. Color the bus drawing a certain color. For example, for Route 1, color the bus blue.

3. Write the bus number on the drawing.

4. Use a different color for the next bus, and so forth.

5. Make "bus tickets" in the "colors" of the bus for each student rider. If student A is going on the Route 1 bus, this ticket would be blue.

6. The driver can collect the tickets each day and save them for reuse.

You will only need to do this for about a week, as each student will learn the driver and the bus on which they are to go. Barring any changes in routes and drivers, these can be used the next year, if laminated.

Which Foot?

Do you have students who do not know which shoe goes on which foot? You can make it simple to know by putting a red sticker dot on the inside of the right shoe. Be sure to inform the parent why the dot is placed in the shoe. The parents can help his or her child focus on this skills, as well.

Left or Right?

Put a colorful letter L, on the left side of the chalkboard. Put a colorful R on the right side of the chalkboard. This helps to cue in students to which is left and which is right.

Miscellaneous Tips

Left or Right? *(cont.)*

Another idea to teach directionality is to use students' hands. Tell them to take both hands and hold them in front of themselves. Have the thumbs pointing at each other, keeping the fingers closed. Tell them to look closely at each hand. The left hand makes the letter L.

Making two hand shapes out of colorful poster board is also a great way to teach the concept of left and right. Make one left hand and one right hand. Put a smiley face on the hands. Have the thumbs of each hand pointing at each other. Below each hand, label left or right.

For some children you may need to put hand shapes on the desks. Cut out small hand shapes from colorful paper. Laminate and attach to the desk, the left hand on the left side and the right hand on the right side.

Need a Spinner?

Make your own. Use a coffee can lid and a large screw. Punch a hole into the center of the coffee can lid. Insert the screw. Using a permanent marker, divide the lid into however many sections you need.

Need More Games?

You can make your own games to add to your center using oilcloth. Make a game board using oil cloth and permanent markers. Just draw your game on the oilcloth and let the students play. One easy game to make would be tic-tac-toe. Use small counting bears as markers. The markers would vary in size according to how large of a tic-tac-toe game is made.

The game boards are easy to store as they will just roll up. Keeping them clean is no problem, either. Use a damp cloth and wipe off.